£25.00

D0504621

THE 55-PLUS MARKET
Exploring a golden business opportunity

THE 55-PLUS MARKET
Exploring a golden business opportunity

Editor: Stephan Buck, B.Sc., Ph.D.

McGRAW-HILL BOOK COMPANY

London · New York · St Louis · San Francisco · Auckland · Bogotá
Guatemala · Hamburg · Lisbon · Madrid · Mexico · Montreal
New Delhi · Panama · Paris · San Juan · São Paulo · Singapore
Sydney · Tokyo · Toronto

Published by
McGRAW-HILL Book Company (UK) Limited
MAIDENHEAD · BERKSHIRE · ENGLAND

British Library Cataloguing in Publication Data

The 55-plus market: exploring a golden business opportunity.
1. Great Britain. Consumers: retired persons
I. Buck, Stephan
339.4'7
ISBN 0-07-707308-8

Library of Congress Cataloging-in-Publication Data

The 55-plus market: exploring a golden business
opportunity / editor, Stephan Buck.
p. cm.
Includes bibliographical references.
ISBN 0-07-707308-8
1. Aged as consumers—Great Britain. 2. Aged as consumers—
United States. I. Buck, S. F. (Stephan Frank) II. Title: Fifty-five-
plus market.
HC260.C6A13   1990
658.8'00844—dc20   89-38400 CIP

Typeset by Rowland Phototypesetting Limited
Bury St Edmunds, Suffolk
and printed and bound in Great Britain by
Billing & Sons Ltd, Worcester

Contents

Acknowledgements

Thanks are due to Harold Lind and Tim Lamb for their helpful ideas and suggestions and my secretary, Maria Brusa, for the hard work necessary to complete this book.

Thanks are also due to the following for permission to reproduce copyright material: AGB Research; Age Concern; The American Academy of Advertising; Nick Baker, cartoonist; Broadcasters' Audience Research Board; Central Statistical Office; Channel 4; Emap; Gallup International; Her Majesty's Stationery Office; Joint Industry Committee for National Readership Surveys; London Weekend Television; Ministry of Agriculture, Fisheries and Food; Office of Population Censuses and Surveys; Research Surveys of Great Britain; Saga Holidays; Seven Seas Ltd; Shire Hall Press & Public Relations; Slaymaker Cowley White Ltd; Statistical Office of the European Communities; United Nations; US Bureau of the Census.

Contributors

Stephan Buck, B.Sc., Ph.D.

Stephan Buck is a Main Board Director of AGB Research where he is responsible for research activity. After gaining a Ph.D. in Mathematical Statistics from London University, and a spell as Chief Statistician with an agricultural research institute, he joined AGB shortly after its formation and has been associated with its growth to become the largest market research company in Europe.

He has specialized in the theory and practice of consumer panel research in a number of different sectors including television, groceries, durables and finance and has been responsible for the development, both at home and abroad, of a number of innovative techniques in these areas.

Stephan Buck is Co-editor of the *Journal of the Market Research Society* and author of many papers and articles, some of which are considered the standards in their field. He is a frequent speaker at conferences and seminars.

John Gabriel

John Gabriel is currently Operations Director of Marketing Improvements Research Ltd, where he is concentrating on research about the over-55s.

In 1987 John Gabriel started Third Age Research as the first consultancy in the United Kingdom to specialize in marketing research among those aged over 55 years. He has subsequently spoken at a number of marketing and research seminars on the subject, as well as appearing on Channel 4's *The years ahead* programme and writing various articles. He is also the author of *Third Age—The People* and *Third Age—The Market*, both published in 1988.

Prior to this, he gained experience in marketing management, mainly in the fast-moving consumer goods arena, and has worked in advertising and market research agencies, both in the United Kingdom and abroad, over a period of more than 20 years.

Sally Greengross

Sally Greengross has been with Age Concern England for 12 years and became Director in June 1987. Her earlier background was in lecturing and research and she taught a variety of professional groups, particularly in the field of health and social services. She is Joint Chairman of the Board of the Age Concern Institute of Gerontology at King's College (London University), a member of the Standing Advisory Committee on Transport for Disabled and Elderly People and a Fellow of The Royal Society of Health.

She writes, lectures and broadcasts frequently both here and in other countries on a wide range of issues concerning policy and practice relating to older people.

She is Joint Co-ordinator of 'Eurolink-Age' a European Community-wide organization working with politicians, administrators and older peoples' organizations at a European level, and International Vice President of the International Federation on Ageing with responsibility for its European office. The IFA is a world-wide non-governmental organization recognized by the main United Nations bodies and agencies, including the World Health Organization which she frequently represents at an International and National level.

Monty Alexander FIPA, MCAM

An innovator in the field of market analysis, strategy and communication, Monty Alexander's first career was in advertising, as Chairman and Creative Director of his own agency, Alexander-Butterfield, and later as board member of a large British advertising agency group.

He left the agency scene to widen his scope into creative marketing, specializing in new product development and corporate and brand repositioning.

Monty Alexander has won a number of marketing, research and advertising awards, including a Cannes gold medal for television advertising. He and his partner won the Market Research Society Award for best presentation with their paper on 'Cultural class' at the 1989 annual conference.

As well as his own consultancy work, he is a Founder Director of the Social Futures Unit, a Director of Semiotic Solutions and a Partner in Marketing to the Third Age. He is a Fellow of the Institute of Practitioners in Advertising and a Member of Communication Advertising and Marketing. He is a past Council Member of the Advertising Creative Circle.

Rena Bartos

Rena Bartos is President of the Rena Bartos Company, and is a consultant and author concerned with communications and consumer issues.

She was formerly a Senior Vice-President and Director of Communications at the J. Walter Thompson Company, and has also been Research Representative on the Creative Plans Board of McCann-Erickson, Director of Research at the Fletcher-Richards Agency, and Associate Research Director at Marplan.

Rena Bartos has won a number of industry awards, and has lectured and consulted throughout the world on the marketing implications of the changing role of women. She is the author of numerous books and articles, the latest being *Marketing to Women: A Global Perspective* (Heinemann, 1989).

The professional organizations with which she is involved include The Advertising Research Foundation (past Chairwoman), The Advertising Educational Foundation (Board of Directors), Advertising Women of New York (past President), The Committee of 200, The Gannett Center for Media Studies, Columbia University, and The Roper Center for Public Opinion Research.

Peter Sleight

Peter Sleight gained grocery brand marketing experience with Cavenham Foods, Unicliffe and RHM Foods, including selling and new product development experience.

He joined Allen Brady & Marsh, the London advertising agency, as Head of Marketing in 1977, joining the ABM board in 1979.

After a spell at CACI as Head of Consultancy, Peter joined Gurmukh Singh to help set up Pinpoint Analysis Limited, which opened its doors in January 1983. He is a director of the company.

Bernard Bennett

Bernard Bennett is Controller of Research at London Weekend Television. An Economics graduate of University College, London, he has held positions at Television Audience Measurement (TAM), Southern Television and Trident, Yorkshire and Tyne Tees. He is a member of several BARB committees.

Abbreviations

AGB	AGB Research
BARB	Broadcasters Audience Research Board
FES	Family Expenditure Survey
GHS	General Household Survey
JICNARS	Joint Industry Committee for National Readership Surveys
LWT	London Weekend Television
NFS	National Food Survey
NRS	National Readership Survey
OPCS	Office of Population Censuses and Surveys
RSGB	Research Surveys of Great Britain
TOM	Television Omnibus Monitor

Social class classifications

A	High managerial, administrative or professional
B	Intermediate managerial, administrative or professional
C1	Supervisory, clerical, junior administrative or professional
C2	Skilled manual workers
D	Semi-skilled and unskilled manual workers
E	State pensioners, widows, casual and lowest grade earners

1
Introduction
Dr Stephan Buck

Some years ago, a British newspaper advertised itself with the slogan 'all human life is here'. I was rather doubtful as to how accurately that thought described the newspaper concerned, which always seemed to me to concentrate rather heavily on a limited number of human activities, but I believe it could be used to describe the scope of the marketing business. Almost everything that happens in the world is of potential relevance to marketing, and many apparently unrelated trends can provide major opportunities or threats.

To give just one example, towards the end of the 1950s in most developed countries, a combination of high post-war birth rates, full employment, rapidly increasing prosperity and a loosening of social and sexual mores opened up the teenage market, which had scarcely existed previously, but which became the dominant influence on marketing during the 1960s and 1970s, and which, as we shall see in the later chapters of this book, still largely affects the thinking of most marketing people. Of course, this is now obvious, perhaps too obvious, but the best marketers were those who saw the changes early and grasped their opportunities.

For a variety of reasons, some of which we discuss later, marketers have, by and large, tended to ignore anyone over 60 years of age, except in a limited number of product fields which are perceived as the province of the old and the decayed. If anything, this tendency has strengthened over the past few decades, being the other side of the coin of increasing interest in the teenage market. However, there are now signs that this long period of marketing indifference to one-third of the adult population is beginning to change. There is increasing discussion about the purchasing power of older people, and the group is even being given childish acronyms (such as 'Glams' and 'Woopies'), a sure sign that the advertising community is beginning to pay attention. This process is still further advanced in the United States, as Rena Bartos discusses in Chapter 8, which augurs well for further developments on this side of the Atlantic. Nevertheless, it is doubtful if many people involved in marketing have considered the full implications of the social changes now taking place which affect the position of older people.

One can isolate three factors which have a bearing on this; one is, to some extent, a matter of opinion, but the other two are objective. The first is a decline in the cult of youth, which has played such a major part in our culture over the past few decades. At present, the pendulum appears to be swinging, at least to some extent, towards a more hierarchical society, which places a higher value on age and experience than on youth and spontaneity. There is considerable evidence for this swing, and I feel there is general acceptance that a move in this direction has taken place, but its extent is open to question and, as with any change in intellectual fashion, it is impossible to be certain how long it will last. The intelligent marketer should take account of this movement, but he should regard it with a certain degree of wariness and should monitor its progress continuously by whatever market research methods seem most appropriate.

The second development is, in one sense, well known to marketers, but they have rarely analysed its effect on different age groups. This is the change in the pattern of wealth as most developed countries become increasingly prosperous. It was pointed out many years ago that both the distribution and the amount of wealth within society was changing. Until recently, and even now in underdeveloped countries, wealth distribution could be regarded as a triangle with a narrow apex, where a few people were very wealthy, a few more were comfortably off and the great majority lived near or below the poverty line. In developed countries at present, the situation is quite different. The picture of wealth distribution is no longer triangular but, rather, is diamond-shaped, with a small number of very poor people at the bottom, the great majority reasonably comfortably off in the middle of society and a much wider triangle on top where a relatively high number of people have a considerable amount of wealth. It can be argued, I think rightly, that this picture has formed the basis of our consumer society over the past 30 years, where, increasingly, a large proportion of the population can afford what would once have been regarded as luxuries for the few. But within this diamond-shaped distribution of prosperity, there are marked differences by age and, at least until recently, these have been either ignored or largely misinterpreted.

It is certainly true that the poor group at the bottom of the diamond shape contains a relatively high proportion of old people. This is well known and, indeed, most social discussion on the aged has dwelt on the problems of this segment of the population and on what society can do to alleviate them. But it is equally true that older people also preponderate in the upper part of the diamond. It may well always have been true that most of the richest members of society were relatively old, although for purposes of mass marketing, this was largely irrelevant when wealth was confined to the very few. But in a society where wealth is growing rapidly or, to put it in diagrammatic terms, the upper triangle is continually widening, the make-up of the upper triangle becomes increasingly important, and thus the high proportion of older people in that group should become increasingly notice-able to marketers. While it is not surprising that the old are beginning to be noticed, it is surprising that the poverty of some old people has for so long obscured the wealth of many.

The final, and in the long term perhaps the most important, development which ought to suggest a marketing reconsideration of the aged, is based on purely demographic factors. Unfortunately, although the statistics are there, the interpretation is not always simple.

We can start with a paradox for anyone making a case for the growing importance of the old. It is a statistical certainty that the proportion of old people in the *world's* population at present is *lower* than ever before. To see why this should be the case and what relevance it has for British marketers, we need to look more closely at the way in which demographic changes generally, and population growth in particular, have taken place.

The human population has been increasing for as far back as records can take us but, until recently, the growth has been very slow and capable of reversal, for a time at least, by such disasters as the Bubonic plague of the fourteenth century. While growth was slow, the proportion of different age groups in the population changed very little over time.

The grand change occurred in Europe and North America around 1800, when population began to increase very rapidly. The cause of this increase was not a higher birth rate, or even a much greater longevity of people who reached middle age, but, rather, the much higher survival rate of the young. The simple statistical result of this change was that countries undergoing rapid population growth saw the proportion of old people in the population declining rapidly as more and more young people were born and survived, a situation which is currently taking place in the rest of the world and which accounts for the decline of the old in the population share.

However, subsequent to the change in the survival rate of the young, populations tend to stabilize as the birth rate falls, a stage now reached in the developed countries. If this trend continues long enough, the proportion of the old in the population begins to rise. This is already happening in the majority of European countries, and there seems little doubt that most developed countries will follow the same path. The increase in the old as a percentage of the population has been relatively modest up to now in the United Kingdom. But figures provided in Chapter 2 show that the pro-portion of the old will begin to rise rapidly during the early years of the next century.

It is the purpose of this book to put the older age group into a context which marketers should find helpful. Though designed for the British market, the book broadens its context since what applies to the United Kingdom applies, to a greater or lesser extent, to almost every other developed country. The important fact for marketers in the United Kingdom is that the longer-term trends favour the older age groups both in terms of wealth and of numbers. Marketers should therefore look carefully at this market, whose significance is only just beginning to become apparent to many people. There is much to be gained from a more innovative approach to marketing for an ageing population since there is little doubt that this is where a golden business opportunity exists.

2
The size and nature of the ageing population
John Gabriel

Introduction

The first necessity for any marketing exercise is to establish a factual basis. How large is the population of older people and what can be said about their relevant social and economic characteristics?

John Gabriel uses the large number of relevant statistics available to flesh out a picture of the position of the old, with particular reference to the United Kingdom.

For many people, even the mention of the word 'demographics' conjures up a picture of page after page of tightly packed figures that appear to have meaning only to statisticians. They take a quick look and pass on to more interesting and relevant things. For the reader of this book who has, by virtue of reading it, more than a passing interest in that one-third of our population who are at, or are in sight of, their retirement I would suggest that you persevere. The figures that we give are generally broad ones and are intended only to highlight the main points. A mass of further information is available from a variety of other sources and even a cursory reading of this will provide you with fascinating insights. What we present here is provided, above all, to stimulate thoughts about what is happening both in the broader social contexts and in the particular markets in which you are personally interested.

1. The world

One of the inevitable difficulties found in dealing with statistics from a variety of countries is that they are compiled to meet differing needs. They are also compiled with varying degrees of sophistication and are reported on at different times. None the less, there is a degree of comparability that can be applied to demonstrate the sizes and natures of those sections of the population who are older than 65 years.

The best source of comparable international demographics appears to be the *UN Demographic Yearbook* and the figures that are discussed here are based on the 1986 edition (Table 2.1). On a worldwide basis about 6 per cent of the world's population of nearly 5 billion people are aged 65 years or older. At first sight, this doesn't seem to be a very attractive proposition to marketers, even though it represents nearly 300 million people. It is only when one begins to turn the magnification of the microscope up a little that some patterns begin to emerge.

Three of the macro regions have a very disproportionate section of their populations who are aged 65 years and over. These are the so-called modern, or first world, areas of Europe, the United States and the Union of Soviet Socialist Republics. Europe comprises some 10 per cent of the world's total population, yet it has over 21 per cent of the total number of over-65s. In the case of North America, the figures are 5 per cent and 10 per cent respectively. The Union of Soviet Socialist Republics has 6 per cent of the world's total population, yet has 9 per cent of all the over-65s. So these three regions account for 40 per cent of the world's over-65s, but only 21 per cent of its total population.

At the other end of the scale are the regions that include many of the so-called underdeveloped countries of the world. In Africa, with 11 per cent of the total population, there are only 6 per cent of the over-65s, yet 15 per cent of the under-15s. The whole region of South Asia accounts for

Table 2.1 Estimates of population and its percentage distribution by age for the world and macro regions (population in millions)

	All ages	−15		65+	
			%		%
World total	4837	1613	33	286	6
Africa	555	250	45	17	3
North America	264	58	22	30	11
Latin America	405	153	38	18	4
East Asia	1250	364	29	71	6
South Asia	1568	608	39	61	4
Europe	492	103	21	61	12
Oceania	25	7	28	2	8
Union of Soviet Socialist Republics	279	69	25	26	9

Source: *UN Demographic Yearbook*, 1986

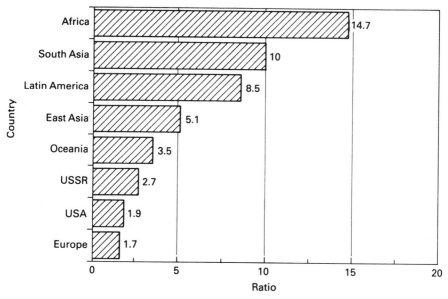

Fig. 2.1 Ratio of under-15s to over-65s—1985 population estimates (*Source: UN Demographic Yearbook*, 1986)

nearly one-third of the world's total population yet has about one-fifth of the over-65s, and nearly 40 per cent of the under-15s.

The disparities are accentuated when one looks at the ratio of the under-15s to the over-65s (Fig. 2.1). In the most developed regions, Europe and North America, there are slightly less than two people aged under 15 years for every person aged over 65 years. In Africa the ratio is nearly 15 younger people to each older one. In South Asia and Latin America the ratios are approximately 10 young to 1 old.

The above figures highlight the enormous contrast that exists between the demographics of the most developed countries and the rest of the world. It also raises many questions that impinge on the future of Europe in the not too distant future. In a continent such as Africa, where nearly half the total population of some 555 million is aged less than 15 years and where a very high birth rate exists, a major problem arises in terms of employment for these new generations. Massive industrial investment is likely to be required from those nations which currently have an industrial base, in those nations which have the raw materials. Yet is this going to be acceptable to the emerging nations who have their own aspirations for relative self-sufficiency and who may be sensitive to what they may perceive as a sort of pseudo-colonial status relationship to the industrial nations? Is a schism likely to develop between producer and consumer nations? With the increasing populations of the underdeveloped nations what is the attitude of the young going to be towards the old who have retired and are now no longer productive? Are they going to be prepared to support them, or will they feel that the old are worthless parasites with nothing to contribute? These are important questions for politicians and sociologists and as such are outside the scope of this book whose concern is with marketing in the short-to-medium term.

2. Europe

On examining population figures for the 12 European Community (EC) countries (based on Eurostat figures), we find a projected growth in total population from a level of 292 million in 1965 to 331 million at the turn of the century, an increase of 13 per cent. A fall to 316 million by the year 2025 is projected. In marked contrast to this fall in total population, the numbers of the over-65s are projected to double between 1965 and 2025, from 32 million to 64 million. Not only will the numbers of old people double, but their proportion of the total population will also double, from a level of 11 per cent to 20 per cent (Table 2.2).

There are some major differences in the growth rates for individual countries within the Community. For example, the over-65 population of Ireland is projected to show no change over the 60-year period, while that

Table 2.2 Percentage of populations aged 65 and over (actual 1965–85; projected to 2025)

Year	1965	1975	1985	1995	2005	2015	2025
Euro-12	11	13	13	15	16	18	20
Federal Republic of Germany	12	14	15	16	19	22	25
France	12	13	13	15	16	18	21
Italy	10	12	13	16	18	19	21
Netherlands	10	11	12	13	14	17	21
Belgium	13	14	14	16	17	18	21
Luxemburg	12	13	13	13	14	15	17
United Kingdom	12	14	15	16	16	17	19
Ireland	11	11	10	10	9	10	11
Denmark	12	13	15	16	15	19	21
Greece	9	12	13	14	16	16	17
Spain	9	10	12	14	15	16	17
Portugal	8	10	12	13	14	14	16

Source: Eurostat Demographic and Labour Force Analysis (1988)

for the Federal Republic of Germany will more than double, until one in four of its population is aged 65 years or more. The next highest levels of growth are projected for Italy and the Netherlands, which will both more than double their proportions of older people, while those of Portugal, Spain and Greece will effectively double.

The proportions of the populations that are projected to be over 65 years of age in the year 2025 show a clear pattern. Half the countries will have more than one out of five of their populations aged over 65 years, five of the remainder will have at least one out of six aged over 65 years and Ireland, with one in ten, is the odd one out.

Another interesting comparison is the time span taken for the levels of the over-65s to increase by half from the base year of 1965. Portugal achieved this level by 1985, while Italy, Greece and Spain are projected to do so by 1995. The Federal Republic of Germany should have done so by 2005, yet France, the Netherlands and Denmark will only do so by 2015, and Belgium and the United Kingdom only by 2025. Luxemburg should be there soon after 2025, but Ireland is not likely to reach that level for many, many years.

The variations in declining birth rates and increasing life expectancies have been the major contributors to these changes in emphasis within the populations of the different countries.

Another element that makes the older sectors of the population of particular interest and importance to marketers is the increasing tendency for people to retire earlier. With their increased life expectancies and their generally higher standards of wealth they become attractive, spending customers for even longer.

This earlier retirement is particularly marked among men. The acceleration in early retirement is shown graphically in Fig. 2.2. In all the nine countries shown (Greece, Spain and Portugal were not members of the Community in 1975 when the benchmark study was undertaken), the percentage of men aged 60 years who were economically active in 1985 is significantly less than it was in 1975. In some countries the decreases have been very marked. For example, in Luxemburg there was a decrease from 69 per cent economically active in 1975 down to 24 per cent in 1985. Other countries to show large decreases are France, from 71 per cent down to 33 per cent, the Federal Republic of Germany, from 81 per cent to 51 per cent, and Belgium, from 67 per cent to 36 per cent. The Netherlands, Denmark and the United Kingdom have all shown decreases of over 20 per cent in economically active 60-year-old men.

Despite these decreases there are still significant differences in the levels of economic activity throughout the Community. For example, three out of four men aged 60 years are still economically active in Ireland, compared

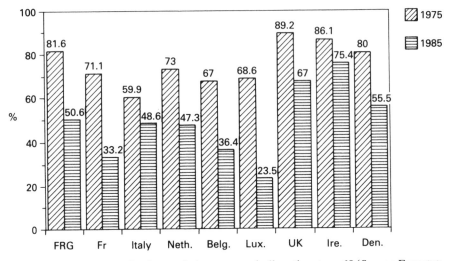

Fig. 2.2   Percentage of male populations economically active at age 60 (*Source*: Eurostat Demographic and Labour Force Analysis, 1988)

with two out of three in the United Kingdom, one out of three in France and one out of four in Luxemburg.

While there is some talk of people retiring much earlier than has previously been the norm, the levels of men who are economically active at age 55 is still high. Belgium has the lowest level at 72 per cent, compared to 90 per cent for the United Kingdom. Even so, there has been an increase in these levels of earlier retirement, ranging from 16 per cent in Belgium and 12 per cent in France, to 3 per cent in Denmark and Ireland.

In overall terms it would appear that the Danes and Irish work longest, with over one out of three men still economically active at the age of 65 years, which contrasts with under 10 per cent for the Benelux countries, and 11 per cent for the Federal Republic of Germany and France.

With these figures in mind, consideration must be given to the impact that the introduction of the Single Community in 1992 will have on the employment and retirement practices of individual member countries. It seems more likely that people in the United Kingdom will fall into line with some of their continental counterparts and retire earlier, rather than the other way round. If this does happen there will be even more retired people in the United Kingdom and the need to understand their needs and aspirations will be even greater.

3. United Kingdom

3.1 Population

Despite popular mythology to the contrary, the population projections prepared for the government, show relatively little change in the total numbers of those aged over 55 years until around the turn of the century. In fact, there is a slight projected fall from the level of 14.8 million in 1986 to a level of 14.5 million in 1996. The level then begins to climb, returning to the 1986 level in 2001 and then climbing to 18.1 million in the year 2021 (Fig. 2.3). Even though the growth in this portion of the population is not as immediate as may have been painted, growth over the period from 1986 to 2021 is of the order of 22 per cent.

If one now looks at the over-55s as a proportion of the total population, they comprised slightly over one-quarter in 1986. This level also remains virtually static until the turn of the century and then climbs until the over-55s represent some 31 per cent of the total population by 2021. Again an impressive proportion, and growth.

When one considers their proportions in the adult (over 16 years) population, the importance of the over-55s becomes even clearer. In 1986 they accounted for 32.9 per cent of the adult population, with these figures projected to jump to 34.3 per cent by 2006 and to 38.5 per cent by 2021. It is a brave, or perhaps foolish, marketer who ignores so large a proportion of

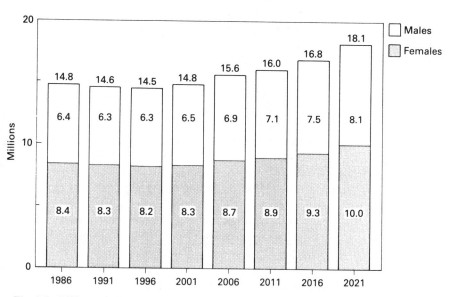

Fig. 2.3   UK population projections—all 55+ (*Source*: *Population Projections*, HMSO, Series PP 2.13)

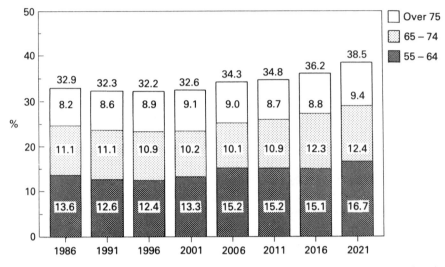

Fig. 2.4   UK population projections—all 55+ as a percentage of all adults (16+) (*Source: Population Projections*, HMSO, Series PP 2.13)

buyers (Fig. 2.4). It is easy enough to talk of the over-55s as one group, but it is apparent to all that there are marked differences in the numbers, and proportions, of variously aged people within this large block.

When we look at the oldest people, i.e. those aged over 75 years, we find that there is projected growth in their total numbers from 1986 until the turn of the century. There were 3.7 million in 1986 and there are projected to be 4.1 million in 2001. The figures stay reasonably constant at that level and only show growth again between 2016 and 2021 when they reach 4.4 million (Table 2.3). This sort of growth pattern is markedly different from that predicted for the youngest and largest subgroup, those aged between 55 and 64 years. This group's numbers of 6.1 million in 1986 fall to 5.6 million in 1996. From then on there is strong growth to a level of 7.0 million in 2011 and then to 7.8 million in 2021.

The other age group here, the 65–74-year-olds, again show a different pattern. There is a constant 5.0 million between 1986 and 1991 which then declines steadily to a level of 4.6 million in 2006 and thereafter increases quite quickly, getting back to its 1986 level by 2011. From then it grows by about 0.7 million within the next five years to reach a level of 5.8 million by 2021.

In summary, the age group for which growth is projected in the immediate future, up to 1996, is the over-75 group, where the gain is of the order of 0.3 million. It is within the youngest of the groups, the 55–64-year-olds, that there is a real decline in numbers of around 0.5 million. There is minimal change within the 65–74-year-old group over the next 10 years.

As is well known, women tend to live longer than men, so that within all the subgroups there are more women than men. The differences become greater as the ages increase. Among the 55–64-year-olds there are 1.1 women to every man, while among the 65–74-year-olds, the ratio is 1.27, and among the over-75s the ratio is 2.0. The above figures are all based on the actual figures for 1986. However, if one looks at the projections up to 2021, it becomes apparent that the differential mortality rate begins to narrow and the ratios of women to men start to decline. Among the youngest group it falls to an almost parity level of 1.05 women to each man. For the 65–74-year-olds it falls to about the 1.2 mark, while among the oldest group it falls to 1.75 women to each man.

3.2 Life expectations

Some of the figures provided in the preceding paragraph have indicated that people, men especially, are going to live longer. This is reinforced when one looks at the expectation of life figures shown in Table 2.4. A male born in the 1950–2 period could expect to live for 66.2 years, while a male born some 30

Table 2.3 UK population projections—millions (mid-1983 based)

	1986	1991	1996	2001	2006	2011	2016	2021
55–64								
Males	2.9	2.8	2.7	2.9	3.3	3.4	3.4	3.8
Females	3.2	3.0	2.9	3.1	3.5	3.6	3.6	4.0
Total	6.1	5.7	5.6	6.0	6.9	7.0	7.0	7.8
65–74								
Males	2.2	2.2	2.2	2.1	2.1	2.3	2.6	2.6
Females	2.8	2.8	2.7	2.6	2.5	2.7	3.1	3.2
Total	5.0	5.0	4.9	4.7	4.6	5.0	5.7	5.8
75+								
Males	1.2	1.3	1.4	1.4	1.5	1.5	1.5	1.6
Females	2.4	2.6	2.6	2.7	2.7	2.6	2.6	2.8
Total	3.7	3.9	4.0	4.1	4.1	4.1	4.1	4.4
All 55+								
Males	6.4	6.3	6.3	6.5	6.9	7.1	7.5	8.1
Females	8.4	8.3	8.2	8.3	8.7	8.9	9.3	10.0
Total	14.8	14.6	14.5	14.8	15.6	16.0	16.8	18.0

Note: Figures may not add due to rounding
Source: *Population Projections 1983–2023*, HMSO, Series PP 2.13

Table 2.4   UK expectation of life at certain ages

	Males	(1) (2)		Females	(1) (2)	
	1950–52	1970–72	1983–85	1950–52	1970–72	1983–85
Age						
0	66.2	68.7	71.8	71.2	75.0	77.6
10	59.1	60.5	62.8	63.6	66.5	68.4
20	49.5	50.8	53.0	53.9	56.6	58.6
30	40.2	41.3	43.4	44.4	46.9	48.7
40	30.9	31.8	33.8	35.1	37.3	39.1
50	22.2	22.9	24.7	26.2	28.2	29.7
55	18.3	18.9	20.5	21.9	23.9	25.3
60	14.8	15.2	16.7	17.9	19.8	21.2
65	11.7	12.0	13.3	14.2	16.0	17.3
70	9.0	9.4	10.4	10.9	12.4	13.7
79	6.7	7.2	7.9	8.0	9.4	10.5

Notes: (1) England and Wales only; (2) provisional
Source: Eurostat Demographic Statistics

or so years later, in 1983–5, could expect to live for 71.8 years, an additional five-and-a-half years. A female born in the 1983–5 period could expect to live six-and-a-half years longer than one born in 1950–2.

While the above figures are interesting, and appealing to those born in the 1980s, the more pertinent ones relate to those who have reached a more mature age. The male who was 55 years old in the 1983–5 period could expect to live for another 20.5 years, an increase of 2.2 years on someone aged 55 in 1950–2. A male who was 70 years old in 1983–5, however, would only have gained 1.4 years on the man aged 70 in 1950–2.

For women, the gains are even greater. A woman who was 55 years old in 1983–5 could expect to live for another 25.3 years, which is 4.8 years longer than a man of the same age, and 3.4 years longer than the woman who was 55 years old in 1950–2. The older woman also has greater expectations. The 70-year-old in 1983–5 can expect to live for another 13.7 years, 3.3 years longer than a man of the same age, and 2.8 years longer than a woman who was 70 years old in 1950–2.

The above expectations all contribute to the overall numbers of people who live beyond 55 and 65 and 75 years. These increased expectations also influence the ways in which people approach their Third Age. If people know that they can reasonably expect to live for another 20 or 25 years, they are likely to plan their lives differently than they would if they expected to live for less than 10 more years. Such changes in attitudes, coupled with increased amounts of disposable income and greater asset levels, make these groups that much more attractive to marketers.

3.3 Marital status

Despite the increasing life expectancy discussed in the preceding section, many married men still die before their wives (Fig. 2.5). Such a toll means that the proportion of married people declines with increasing age. Among the 55–64-year-old group, about three-quarters are married, with this figure falling to around 60 per cent for the 65–74-year-old group. In the whole over-75s group, the figure falls to a level where only one out of three is married. Within this oldest group the levels fall markedly as age increases (Fig. 2.5).

3.4 Households

While the over-55s represent about one out of four of the total population, and one out of three of the adult population, they really come into their own in terms of constituting over 40 per cent of heads of households in the country. This means that they head some 9 million homes.

Many marketers assume that the purchasing levels of households headed by people over 55 years, and especially those over 65 years, are low and can

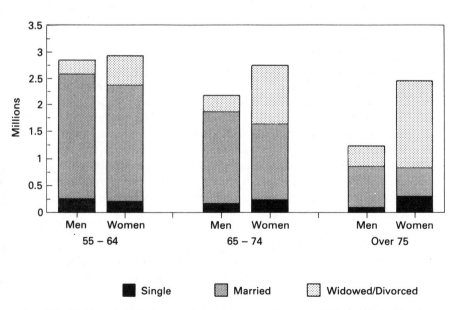

Fig. 2.5 Marital status of over-55s—mid-year estimates, 1987—United Kingdom (*Source*: *Annual Abstract of Statistics*, 1989)

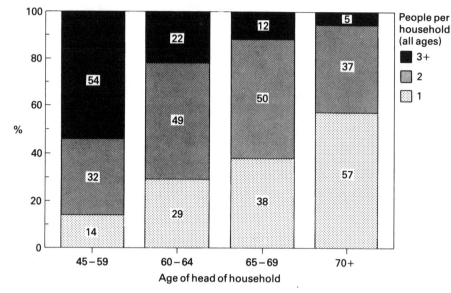

Fig. 2.6 Great Britain—household size (*Source*: OPCS General Household Survey, 1986)

therefore be ignored. What they do not realize is that the *per capita* spending in this group is quite high and that the main reason for lower household spending is that there are fewer people in those households.

In households where the head is aged between 50 and 64 years there is an average of 2.35 people in that household. Where the head of the household is aged between 65 and 74 years the number of people in the household falls to 1.71, and where the head is aged over 75 years the number falls further to 1.45 people (Fig. 2.6). The implications of this are far-reaching. There are many products and appliances and services that are essential for any household regardless of the age of its head. It is likely to be the number of households, rather than the numbers of individuals, that dictates the sizes of many market sectors and this is an area in which the over-55s are very important. This whole topic is covered in much greater detail in Chapter 5.

3.5 Types of dwelling
In recent years, there has been growing awareness that the housing requirements of older people are changing. These changes apply in a number of areas, with the needs of the infirm and less-physically-able elderly getting most coverage in the media. This is largely because of the increasing numbers of the very old (Section 3.2) who are living longer and are in need of continuous attention. Accommodation for the elderly is provided to

some extent by local authorities, although the figures for those aged over 65 years living in such accommodation was, in 1984, only just over the 100 000 level.

There has also been a rapid growth in the private sector provision of accommodation for older people, which has taken a number of forms and ranges from the conversion of large old buildings into flatlets with full nursing facilities available at all times, through flat or townhouse complexes with a central aid/control point, to stand alone bungalows that have been designed to include all possible labour-saving features. The speed with which the better researched and designed developments sell seems to speak for itself in terms of the need for such accommodation.

There is an important division in terms of home ownership that impinges on the current over-55s and, more particularly, the over-65s. In 1984 the level of house ownership among those aged over 65 years was between 45 per cent and 49 per cent, while for those aged between 60 and 64 years it was 56 per cent and among the 45–59-year-olds it was 66 per cent. Thus it is evident that, as time passes, the proportion of the over-55s who are home owners will increase, with all the attendant implications in terms of the products and services that are needed to maintain a home.

On the other hand, the over-70s account for some 41 per cent of all those who rent private unfurnished accommodation. They also account for 30 per cent of the accommodation rented from housing associations or co-operatives. Around 40 per cent of all those aged over 55 years rent their accommodation from a local authority or new town. The polarization of the older population in housing terms reflects the very different economic position between large groups of over-55s.

When one considers that the large majority of the over-55s live in one- or two-person households (60–64-year-olds, 79 per cent; 65–69-year-olds, 87 per cent; over-70-year-olds, 94 per cent) it is not surprising that they tend to live in the smaller types of accommodation, such as flats and bungalows. Of the over-65s some 40 per cent are accommodated thus (Fig. 2.7). Put another way, flats account for about 16 per cent of all accommodation and one-half of those are occupied by those aged over 55 years. For bunga-lows the figures are even greater, with two-thirds being occupied by the over-55s, although bungalows only make up 9 per cent of all available accommodation.

3.6 Social grade

While the social grade definitions may leave something to be desired, they do give some indications of income, and thus of possible lifestyle.

For a marketer new to these figures it is easy to write off the over-55s as more than half are classified in Classes D or E. This is not a wise thing to do,

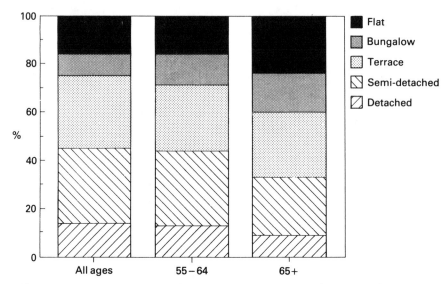

Fig. 2.7 United Kingdom—types of dwellings occupied (*Source*: AGB Market Information)

especially among those aged between 55 and 64 years. On examination of Fig. 2.8 one can see that the proportions of this age group match the national figures for all the classifications quite well. The greatest disproportion of D, Es exists among the older members of the over-65 group. These people are living basically on state pensions, or on the savings that they made for retirement in the days prior to inflation. Many were not able to make personal provision for their retirement and consequently have had to make do. This has left them with little discretionary spending power and has thus reduced their appeal to marketers. There are among them the genuinely severely financially disadvantaged, who are sometimes suffering from real poverty and are among those most often associated in the minds of marketers with 'the old'. They tend to be the most elderly and, to be brutally honest, are the ones who have the least years to live. They are thus of least interest and business concern to marketers. However, in looking at the importance of the over-55s within the different social definitions, we find that they account for over 30 per cent of Classes A and B, 36 per cent of the Class C1 and 29 per cent of Class C2.

If the marketer takes a conservative stance and decides that members of Classes D and E are too poor to be considered, this still leaves some eight million people in the A, B, C groupings. This is, in itself, a substantial market and is well worth further investigation, especially as many of these people have considerable wealth at their disposal.

(At this point it is, perhaps, worth issuing a small caveat in terms of those social classifications as they are applied in market research. For those who are commissioning research into this over-55s area, it may be worthwhile ensuring that the interviewers involved are actively aware that not all those who are 'retired' should be automatically classified as 'E'. Instances have been noted of retired people with substantial private pensions being incorrectly classified in this way, and thus wrongly lumped together with those whose only source of income is their state pension.)

3.7 Internal migration

Another image of old people depicts them retiring from their working environment in the big industrial cities to cottages at the seaside. This is partly true, but a closer examination of internal migration figures (Table 2.5) shows some interesting localized variations. Of the standard regions, Yorkshire and Humberside, and the North and West Midlands showed virtually no net change in 1987 in their over-60-year-old populations. The largest gains came in the South West, particularly Dorset, Devon, Cornwall and Isles of Scilly and Somerset. Both the East Midlands, especially Lincolnshire, and East Anglia showed net gains, while Greater London had the largest outflow of any region. These figures may show a net migration away from the big cities but there are still many thousands of over-60-year-olds moving into them. This locational element is discussed in more detail in Chapter 9.

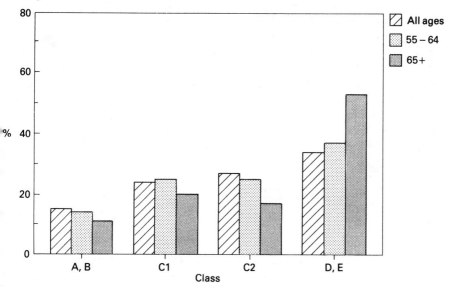

Fig. 2.8   United Kingdom—social class by age (*Source*: AGB)

Table 2.5   Movements between Family Practitioner Committee areas in England and Wales during 1987 (thousands). Age 60 and over

Standard regions	In	Out	Net inflow
North	3.9	3.0	+0.9
Yorkshire and Humberside	7.2	5.8	+1.4
East Midlands	11.2	6.4	+4.8
East Anglia	11.8	4.8	+7.0
South East	13.5	43.0	−29.5
Greater London	6.7	34.6	−27.9
Remainder of South East	31.1	32.7	−1.6
South West	21.9	10.6	+11.2
West Midlands	9.0	7.3	+1.6
North West	6.2	8.3	−2.1
Wales	8.5	3.9	+4.6

Source: *Key Population and Vital Statistics*, 1987, OPCS

4. Conclusion

From the foregoing it is apparent that the over-55s sector of the market is a highly significant one, both within the European community, and within the United Kingdom. It is important, however, to move beyond the basic statistics and to look in more detail at the sorts of people who make up the older market; this is undertaken in the next chapter.

References and recommended reading

European Communities, Statistical Office, *Eurostat Demographic and Labour Force Analysis*, Luxembourg
HMSO, Central Statistical Office, *Annual Abstract of Statistics*, London
Ibid., *Family Expenditure Survey*, London
HMSO, Office of Population Censuses and Surveys, *General Household Survey*, London
Ibid., *Key Population and Vital Statistics*, London
HMSO, series: *Population Projections*, London
UN Demographic Yearbook, United Nations, New York

3
Portraits of the over-55s in the United Kingdom
John Gabriel

Introduction

The preceding chapter was primarily concerned with establishing the size and movements of the over-55s population, both historically and geographically. Simple counting of this kind inevitably treats all over-55s as equal which, as common sense and the subsequent chapters of the book will demonstrate is, of course, not true from a marketing point of view. To point us in the direction of sensible segmentation, John Gabriel takes the findings of a significant qualitative study to develop a series of typologies that differentiate the over-55s. He finds and labels eight such segments of this population and provides a thumb-nail sketch of each. Readers will, I am sure, recognize friends, colleagues, or even themselves, among these cameos.

Let's start with a definition of the term 'Third Age'. This definition has been taken from the French philosophy that 'the first age is for learning, the second for working and the third for LIVING'. We are interested in those who have reached that point in their lives where they can begin to concentrate on the things that please them. They have probably paid off their mortgages, their children have left home, or are independent, and they now have time for themselves. It is now time for them to live. While there is obviously no specific age for this process to start, we decided on 55 years as being the threshold age.

Why aren't marketers paying attention to these people? Marketers are, by and large, aware, intelligent, information-oriented managers, so why are they apparently blind to the Third Agers? One of the probable reasons is that the Third Agers are not visually conspicuous. Does this mean that they are invisible? Partly, yes (particularly to those who are younger, as are most marketing managers, advertising planners and creatives). If you doubt this then try a little test. The next time you are in a high street, railway station or some other crowded place, look at the people around you and see if you can guess how old each is. Sounds so simple doesn't it? The young are reasonably easy, up to age 25 very easy. From then until about the mid-forties fairly easy, but over that sort of age it starts to get more difficult. Again, you may imagine that to put an accurate age to the very old is easy, but is that grey haired lady 70, or 80, or 90 years, or then perhaps only 58 years? At first you probably won't even be within five years of the right age. From this little test you will understand why the Third Agers don't stand out and therefore aren't often uppermost in anybody's mind.

Who are these Invisible People? What are they like? What makes them tick now? What made them the way they are? These were some of the questions that research set out to answer. The intention was to see if it was possible to develop a series of typologies for those aged 55 years and over, and to see what were the factors that differentiate between them and that they have in common. This exercise allowed us to consider them as different groups of people and to begin to understand how to communicate with them.

This study involved a series of discussion groups that were held across the country in both urban and rural areas. The initial hypothesis, that age would be the major determinant of attitudes, led to the first groups being recruited on the basis of three age bands: 55–64, 65–74 and 75 years and over. It soon became apparent that age is not the key determinant and that mental outlook and attitude is. There were many mental attitudes held in common across many different ages, rather than the age dictating the attitudes. This was manifest, in simple terms, by the numbers of those in their 80s who were very 'young' in their approach to life, and by those in their 60s who were 'old' in theirs.

The research was carried out primarily among Classes A, B and Cs as these are the groupings of greatest interest to marketers.

A total of eight typologies were developed from the groups and are being used as broad guidelines to Third Agers. These typologies are not carved in tablets of stone. There is overlap between the attitudes that go to make up the typologies, with individual Third Agers having amounts of several different typologies in their personal make-up. Individuals do not necess-arily stay mainly in one typology throughout their Third Age. External factors can have major influences on their attitudes, and over a 30-year period peoples' requirements from life are likely to change. In fact, there are a number of the typologies which are predominantly transient, with the individual moving into and then out of them. Such migration is often evident after a traumatic event such as the death of the partner.

Also, the typologies do not suddenly become manifest at the age of 55 years. The characteristics begin to develop earlier and are likely to become more entrenched once the Third Age is reached.

There are many marriages in which each partner is of a basically different typology, yet they have sufficient in common to be able to come to a satisfactory compromise. These compromises can be very important as, with a lot more time available in which to satisfy one's own needs, it is very easy for an individual to become extremely self-centred, to the detriment of the long-standing relationship. Probably among the most marked characteristics of people in their Third Age are the increased levels of self-awareness and therefore of self-centredness.

Influences
Third Agers obviously do not suddenly come into their typologies the moment they turn 55 years or when they retire. These have developed over their whole lives and have been, and continue to be, subject to many varied influences, to varying degrees.

There are many factors that have influenced our Third Agers, over which they have had virtually no personal control. (It is important to remember that we are discussing people who were born in 1934 and earlier.) The prime factor has probably been the economic state of the country. Most of our Third Agers were brought up in the depressed economic times of the 1930s when there was enormous unemployment and real hardship. For the majority, life was hard, more of a stage to be got through than enjoyed.

They were then subjected to the rigours and terrors of the Second World War. None of the Third Agers were unaffected by this, regardless of whether they were too young to be actively involved or whether they were involved in either military or other war service. Most of the men lost six or seven years of what should have been the most productive and constructive period of their lives. Many saw active service, with its attendant horrors and privations, although there was a positive aspect for some in that when they saw service overseas they learned something about other peoples. In some, this engendered a desire to travel and a curiosity about the rest of the world. At home, many of the women were drafted into the factories and were taught technical skills which they would never otherwise have been exposed to, and which they have rarely had the opportunity to use since.

After the War came the period of reconstruction, of ration books, and shortages of many commodities and most luxuries. This lasted through the 1940s and well into the 1950s, with consumerism and full shops only really becoming a fact of life in the 1960s. Many Third Agers had thus gone through around 30 years of austerity, by which time they were growing too old or too dispirited, or perhaps too cautious to enjoy the better times. Many were really of the 'doom and gloom' generations rather than the 'boom' generations that have followed.

Knowing that they had to go through their lives under such circumstances makes it easier to understand a number of the attitudes that are common, particularly among the older Third Agers. Attitudes to money for example, were heavily influenced by rarely having enough, so philosophies such as 'neither a lender nor a borrower be' and 'if you can't pay cash don't buy it' were commonplace and have remained among some of the oldest. Among the younger Third Agers these attitudes are less prevalent, and the use of credit cards and buying on credit is frequent.

Another external element which has had enormous influence on Third Agers, and over which they have no effective control, is television. They have lived through the evolution of television since the earliest days of 9 inch black and white sets in large ornate consoles, offering only a few hours of programmes a day, to the current situation where they have a choice of over 20 different channels via satellite, cable or normal transmission, available 24 hours a day, seven days a week. They are avid television watchers (see Chapter 5) and watch on average for over five hours every day. When one combines this heavy viewing with the fact that over three-quarters of the Third Agers had finished their formal schooling by the time they were 16 years old, the enormous effect that television must have in influencing opinions, attitudes and habits becomes apparent. Whether this influence has been used to good or bad effect is a matter of considerable conjecture.

On a personal basis there are three factors that have the most important influences on the way an individual tends to view life. These are health, financial status and marital status.

A person who has been fortunate, or careful, enough to maintain his/her health well into the Third Age is able to achieve much more and to benefit greatly from the Third Age years. The amount a person can do is often dictated by their physical mobility, so the maintenance of basic health is critical. For others a considerable amount of energy, especially emotional, is expended in worrying about their health. This is particularly so when their mobility is under threat. This concern with health takes several different forms. For many men it takes the form of basic exercise, probably in walking the dog, and perhaps in exercises that are specific for particular complaints such as stiff joints. Men are less likely to take to many of the proprietary medicines than are women, who tend to have been heavier users of these products from their middle years onwards. Concern with diet also begins to assume a larger role in their lives, often as a form of health maintenance.

Another of the key criteria in a fulfilled Third Age is the level of financial resources that can be brought to bear upon it. Much of this depends on the degree of preplanning that has gone into working out a successful retirement. For those whose incomes are fixed at a lowish level, or are limited, the stress created in trying to balance their books in order to live within their means is considerable. With the growth in the numbers of people who are retiring with pensions other than the basic state pension, it is likely that this problem may be reduced somewhat. The considerable increase in value of properties over the past decade or so means that many Third Agers are living in homes that are worth well into six figures and are fully paid for. Many of these people are either unable to, or are unaware of how to, release any of these funds, and are subsequently living at considerably lower standards and qualities of life than they need to. These are the asset rich/income poor people. Price increases and the prospects of higher levels of inflation can cause considerable stress to Third Agers, and can lead them to reduce their external activities, with consequent further reductions in their quality of life.

The third of the key personal influences is that of marital status. For many couples retirement is the first time in their married lives in which they have ever actually been together all day for longer than the odd annual holiday. This fact of having a retired husband around the home all day can be a problem for a wife, who may feel that the role that she has established over many years is now under threat. The ability to get on together and to develop a lifestyle that accommodates the aspirations of both partners is very important and needs planning and discussion. As Third Agers get older there is the actuarial likelihood of the husband dying first and leaving his widow to cope with the world on her own. For many this is a worrying time, and they may find themselves not knowing how to handle even such things as the basic domestic finances of paying the rates and electricity bills. These problems, coming on top of the death of their partner, can be very traumatic. The continued contact with family, either children or, increasingly with age, siblings or relatives of the same generation, is also very important in reinforcing the individuals self-esteem. The ability to get in touch with people quickly is also important, especially with the breakdown of the geographically close family units of their youth.

Other areas that also influence attitudes to life include such things as: working background; military service; social activities; access to private or public transport; availability of a telephone (which can literally be a life-line to many); the geographic area in which they live and educational background.

1. The typologies

The eight typologies are outlined below and the main characteristics of each are covered in broad brushstrokes.

Fig. 3.1 The Apathetic (*Source*: Third Age Research)

1.1 The Apathetic

The Apathetic (Fig. 3.1) is a predominantly male typology, most often found in the more industrial areas of the country. He is likely to have been a manual or semi-skilled worker throughout his working life. He feels that he has worked physically hard all through these working years and on his retirement deserves a rest, and he is going to see that he gets one.

During his life things have happened to him rather than his having arranged them, and this is carried through to his retirement. He has probably made neither financial nor emotional preparation for it and when it actually comes he doesn't know what to do about or with it.

He is most likely to be a heavy television watcher, limiting his outside excursions to those he deems to be essential. As one result of this, he often gives the impression of being a somewhat 'grey' person, both in his attitudes and even through to his dress.

This Apathetic mind-set can have disastrous repercussions in that there are many examples of those who have taken this route after retirement becoming so set in their ways that they find no real reason for living. When they reach this stage the chances are that they may not live to see their 70th birthday because they do not have the motivation for doing so.

While the above description is the most common form of Apathetic, there are also those who have fallen into this typology after a particularly traumatic event, such as the death of their partner. For them there is also little reason to go on living but, often through the consideration of others, they move on from here into another stage of their life and a more positive typology.

1.2 The Comfortable

The Comfortable (Fig. 3.2) is probably one of the commoner of the typologies, and can be either male or female. The Comfortables' main characteristic is that they live within well-defined comfort zones. These zones are usually both physical/geographic and emotional, with most of their activities being carried out within a relatively small radius of their homes. While not total homebodies, they tend to be very happy and comfortable in their lives, with their homes acting as life's focal point.

Their lives are likely to include such activities are gardening, embroidery and other comparatively sedentary occupations. They may well become involved in local church, WI or mothers union activities.

When Comfortables do venture away from home they are likely to limit their holiday activities to trips within the country, as they don't like to be away from their homes for more than a few nights at a time. Day trips are popular and there is a strong feeling that 'British is best'. Not for them the

Fig. 3.2 The Comfortable (*Source*: Third Age Research)

exotic foreign foods to be found in the ubiquitous local tandoori restaurant but, rather, roast beef and two veg, or fish and chips.

They have a deep love of their own homes, in which they have probably lived for many years. They will devote a considerable amount of time to developing and maintaining their gardens and to caring for their homes.

The Comfortables are more likely to patronize their local shops than go to the bigger shopping centres or to the larger supermarkets. They feel that they are being taken advantage of by the big chains, who have frequently destroyed their old local shops to make way for the big developments. Shopping trips to the big centres are a major undertaking and are made as infrequently as possible, with this being frequently accentuated by having to use public transport as they have no transport of their own.

One result of this attitude to life is that they tend to be more brand loyal than most other Third Agers. Not for them the experimenting with new brands and products as soon as these come onto the market.

1.3 The Explorer

This is a typology of the single person (Fig. 3.3), predominantly, but by no means exclusively, female, brought about as much by widowhood as anything else. The main driving force is a belief that 'life is for living', so she sets about doing whatever her financial and physical resources will allow.

The Explorer is a great experimenter. She will try new things, be they ballet at the age of 65 years, learning to swim at 60 years, learning to drive or use a computer. She sees her age as no barrier to trying a range of new activities nor to visiting new, or even familiar old, places. She sees both a necessity for, and gets pleasure from, keeping both her mind and body active. There is often a strong orientation to the self, even where a partner is available. She is likely to take trouble to find out about all the concessions that are offered to older people, be these cheap fares on local regional transport or British Rail, special rates for matinees at theatres or being able to act as a model at the local hairdressing school, thereby getting regular, and free, hairdo's.

She is likely to be somewhat contemptuous of her peers who are not prepared to make the effort to find out about available activities and to take advantage of them. However, she will spend time explaining what is available and will happily take advantage of these opportunities with like-minded souls, probably other Explorers.

She is a keen traveller and, where finances and inclination allow, she is to be found in the far corners of the world in such places as the foothills of the Himalayas, on Fishermans Wharf in San Francisco or even on the beach at Ipenema. She is to be found in large numbers throughout the Iberian peninsular and in the Canaries, especially in the so-called off-season times.

Fig. 3.3 The Explorer (*Source*: Third Age Research)

This relative adventurousness spreads to her eating habits where she will both eat, and often cook, what appear to be exotic foreign foods.

For those who are less physically able there is a subgroup called the Mental Explorers. Their energies tend to be channelled into such activities as voracious reading, selective television viewing or maybe even into using a personal computer. The 90-year-old lady who is taking her third degree with the Open University definitely falls into this category!

All the Explorers are survivors. They get a great deal of pleasure from life and see boredom as both unnecessary and as a weakness. Life is for living and they do.

As in the mainstream of their lives the Explorers are keen experimenters with new products and brands. For the numbers who live alone this is often manifest in the ownership, and heavy use, of such products as microwave ovens. In these they are likely to cook some of the new ready-prepared, value-added meals for one.

1.4 The Fearful

If there is an archetypal old person, the portrayal is usually of a 'little grey haired old lady'. This could, in many ways, also be the description of the Fearful (Fig. 3.4). The typology is mostly female and is predominantly found among the older, over-80-year-old, Third Agers.

For her the pace of modern life is too hectic, loud, garish and generally she feels that it is beyond her abilities to cope with adequately. It fills her with fear. She is likely to be found among the more physically frail and often lives on her own. She finds that her mental and physical reactions have become very much slower than they were. These factors make her reluctant to go any further from her home than she has to in order to ensure that she can get through her essential daily routines. She is also reluctant to go into areas with which she is unfamiliar.

The Fearful is concerned about what she sees as her failing health. She is particularly concerned lest she fall, or be in some other way incapacitated so that she is unable to summon help. The apparent decline in community spirit and family closeness increases her feelings of loneliness and fear, thus encouraging her to bolt and chain her front door. She is very rarely found outside her home after dark.

Another area of concern to her is money. She tends to feel that she cannot afford to spend money on herself, or on anything that she sees as luxuries. The arrival of a large rates, telephone, electricity or gas bill can engender in her a real level of fear that she will be unable to pay for it. This attribute can often exist despite there being substantial sums of money in her bank account, or owning a valuable home or having other assets. She is fearful of

Fig. 3.4 The Fearful (*Source*: Third Age Research)

money and was often brought up in an age when money was never the province of women.

In many Fearfuls there is still a fierce degree of independence. Any overt threat to this fills her with dread as she feels that she would no longer be in control of her own life, and that would be an intolerable indignity.

1.5 The Organizer

Currently, the Organizer (Fig. 3.5) is predominantly male, towards the younger end of the Third Age, although as more female executives work their way through the workforce, there are likely to be more female Organizers. The Organizer tends to have a working background of a position of authority in which he has been responsible for organizing a shop-floor, office, company or even a military unit. He has been involved in organizing other people and is firmly convinced that just because he has retired he has not lost the skills and experience of all those working years.

He is eager to put something back into society and is the archetype of the person who gives copiously of his time to charities and voluntary organizations. He derives a great deal of satisfaction from such work whether it is acting as chairman of a local committee or driving a meals-on-wheels van. Many charities and local government organizations would be very much worse off without him.

He is also likely to be an organizer of trips for other Third Agers, or for the disadvantaged. Should he be a resident in a sheltered housing area, he is likely to ensure that there are enough activities arranged so that nobody need be lonely or uninvolved.

He is concerned with people and feels that everybody should get a fair crack of the whip. In many ways he is the 'salt of the earth'.

As a consumer he is likely to be interested in new products that can promise an increase in efficiency, be it mechanical or perhaps a reduction in the preparation and cooking times of foods.

1.6 The Poor Me

This is one of the most transient of the typologies and is usually female (Fig. 3.6). The Poor Me feels frustrated with her life. She has not been able, yet, to come to terms with either the prospect or the reality of retirement, or of her changing roles with her partner or with her family at large. In this phase she feels lost and, probably, unloved. She tends to be at the younger end of the Third Age and often has a lot of innate passion and energy which she feels unable to channel.

For the Poor Me who has worked, there is the tendency to feel that she was forced to retire rather than having done so willingly. She finds that she misses

Fig. 3.5 The Organizer (*Source*: Third Age Research)

the stimulation and companionship of her working environment and now questions her own value as a human being.

She can be turned into a Poor Me by a variety of events. These could be as simple as the fact that her youngest grandchild has now gone to school and she is now no longer needed to babysit or to fetch and carry; or it could be as traumatic as the death of her partner. She has been forced into a situation for which she was unprepared and feels unable to cope. She now feels rather like a ship without a rudder, drifting helplessly at the mercy of any passing wind, over which she has no control.

The male Poor Me has often had early retirement forced upon him. He feels that he has been let down by those in authority, either by his company, by his union or by government. He has a very strong feeling of resentment and self-pity.

For the majority of Poor Me's their stay within this typology is a relatively short one. It tends to give them time to get themselves together and in a frame of mind to face the realities of the world again, in whatever form these now present themselves. This transition process can be helped considerably by understanding friends and relatives who give encouragement and instill a feeling of self-worth into the Poor Me.

1.7 The Social Lion

This typology is often manifest as a couple, although there are many instances of individual male and female Social Lions (Fig. 3.7). The key characteristic of this group is their delight in, and need for, the company of others.

Social Lions are likely to be found in any organization where there are regular meetings, and especially where there is a club house or meeting place. They will be active members of organizations such as golf, tennis, bridge, bowls and social clubs, where they are likely to involve themselves in internal organization and politics.

They are likely to have lived in the same neighbourhood for many years and to have built up a substantial circle of friends and acquaintances. These will be augmented with friends made from within the business world in which they have moved. They will socialize with these friends both in the domestic environment and in restaurants.

Social Lions enjoy travelling, both locally and overseas. They are likely to cover considerably greater mileages in their cars once they have retired than they did previously. A lot of this mileage will be generated by their habit of eating out, which they enjoy and share with like-minded friends whenever possible. They are frequently to be found in the dining rooms of country pubs on weekday lunch times.

They are also likely to devote substantial amounts of time to their

Fig. 3.6 The Poor Me (*Source*: Third Age Research)

Fig. 3.7 The Social Lion (*Source*: Third Age Research)

grandchildren, especially in taking them to interesting and educational places, with the overt intention of improving their general education.

Within their shopping patterns there is a strong element of importance given to the buying of brands that are socially correct, especially when these brands are easily recognizable—a product such as Barbour clothing is an obvious example.

1.8 The Status Quoer

This typology is somewhat more male- than female-oriented (Fig. 3.8). It is characterized by the way in which preparation, both financial and mental, has been made for the retirement years. This is likely to have taken the form of having tried a range of hobbies and activities before retirement so that he could gauge what he wanted to do when he finally had the time. He has thus ensured that the trauma of actual retirement has been reduced and that the status quo is maintained as much as possible in his retired life. He is now just doing more of what he had been dabbling in previously.

The Status Quoer is likely to enjoy DIY-type activities and may well have refurbished his home prior to, or immediately after, retirement. He is also likely to display a strong vein of domesticity by helping his wife with the domestic chores. This is done more to release time for he and his wife to be able to do things together than from any particular love of housework. The female Status Quoer's interests may well include gardening, knitting, embroidery and other crafts.

They both enjoy travelling although they are glad to get home at the end of the trip. Their foreign destinations are likely to be of the less adventurous kind, probably being limited to Europe and the other countries surrounding the Mediterranean.

Status Quoers are reasonably experimental in terms of the products and brands that they buy. This is especially so for products that can be seen to enhance the quality of their lives.

2. Tailpiece

Throughout all the typologies, a few broad generalizations apply. These include the feeling that the 'good old days' were not so good, and that the current times are the best that many people have ever known.

There is often a very strong bond between grandparents and grand-children. This can act as a major motivator for the grandparents, and it encourages them to remain alert and active.

Most Third Agers have a fierce sense of independence and virtually the greatest threat that can be made to them is for their independence to be challenged. The prospect of becoming unable to cope is very demotivating,

Fig. 3.8 The Status Quoer (*Source*: Third Age Research)

and the thought of an Old Peoples' Home is often seen as being only one step away from death, which is the only way out. This is partly why so many of the older Third Agers will tolerate what seem to be appalling conditions rather than give up their independence.

References and recommended reading

Third Age Research, Research Surveys of Great Britain, 'The Market', London, 1988
Ibid., 'The People', London 1988

4
In need of help
Sally Greengross

Introduction

We shall see from the material in subsequent chapters that the over-55s are an extremely polarized segment of the population. At one end of the scale there exist large numbers of older citizens who in absolute and relative terms are well-off and potentially exciting from a marketer's point of view. Indeed, much of this book is devoted to the opportunities that present themselves to marketers in a wide range of product fields and services. But before we turn to this, we need to remember and consider the other end of the scale—the conventional old age pensioner who finds it difficult to cope economically and socially. Sally Greengross takes up this important social issue and describes how Age Concern deals with people in need.

We hear a lot nowadays about the power of elderly people as consumers, and it is true that many older people do have a great deal more spending power than previous generations. However, in our work at Age Concern, we also see the other side of the coin, for there are still a great number of elderly people struggling to get by on very low incomes, and these are the people we are most involved with in our work. An older couple trying to get by on state pensions does not fit easily into the modern view of retired consumers, but they are consumers nevertheless, consumers in a very real sense, not only of food and durable goods, but also of the National Health Service, local social service provisions, leisure facilities and a great many other areas. It is this wider interpretation of 'the consumer' which I wish to concentrate on in this chapter, in order to present a full picture of the position of older consumers in our society.

The structure of society is changing rapidly and older people have a crucial part to play in its future development. Already, there are over 10 million people above retirement age in the United Kingdom—18 per cent of the total population—and this age group will continue to be the fastest growing sector of the population well into the next century. In 1984, on retirement, a woman could expect to live to 81 years and a man to 78.2 years. We have now reached the stage where, because of the trend towards early retirement, many people can contemplate 20, or even 30, years of retired life.

It is wrong to view elderly people as a 'problem group' in society. Older people have a wealth of experience, skills and advice to offer the community; we must learn to recognize this resource and to draw on it as much as possible. Retired people also have the time and the opportunity to try new areas of activity and to learn new skills which in turn increase their activity, which in turn increase their value to society. Age Concern England, which runs many national campaigns, and works through 1000 local groups, is launching a major initiative for 1990—its Golden Jubilee year—to educate key sectors of society about the implications that an ageing population have for us all, and about the challenges and opportunities this presents. We believe that it is essential to foster and develop new levels of awareness in order to ensure that all elderly people can have a dignified and enjoyable later life. The particular needs of vulnerable elderly people, and the problems faced by the significant number of older people who have to cope with such problems as low incomes, poor housing, loneliness, loss of mobility and feelings of isolation must be recognized and addressed by professionals and providers of services in all spheres if we are to achieve this aim.

Perhaps by outlining some of the main areas in which elderly people participate as consumers, I will be able to illustrate some of these fundamental needs and desires, for these are issues to which planners and marketing experts should be turning their attention now, in order to ensure a more satisfactory and fulfilling future for us all.

1. Shopping

To take the subject of shopping first, particularly food shopping, older people are active and regular users of shops. The most recent Family Expenditure Survey statistics show that they do not spend significantly less per head than younger groups.

Obviously, the elderly's patterns and methods of shopping will vary according to personal circumstances, and there are some very crude definitions that can be drawn here: 77 per cent of people aged between 60 and 84 years spend less that £20 per week on food, but in the 55–59 age group this figure drops to 28 per cent. Clearly, the needs of the older retired person will differ from those of the younger retired person. People in the older age range—and particularly at the top end—are more likely to eat less, to shop locally, to buy regularly and in smaller quantities than those people in the younger age group. People who are newly retired are more likely to have better access to transport, and additional income; both factors which will have a considerable influence on their shopping habits.

Access to, and convenience of, shops is a very important point. A trip to the shops can be an exhausting affair, particularly if you are physically frail or suffer from lack of mobility. Many older people may be deterred from visiting their local town centre or shopping centre, not only because of the practical difficulty of getting there, but also because of the lack of awareness of their needs displayed by shopkeepers. At Age Concern we have been running what we consider to be a very important campaign, called 'We Care with a Chair', for several years now. This campaign encourages shopkeepers to display a sticker in their window informing shoppers that a seat is available in the shop if they need it. This simple gesture can make an enormous difference to the shopper at very little inconvenience to the retailer—the chair does not even need to be out all the time, it just needs to be available on request.

Although we have had a very encouraging response to the campaign so far, we would like to see the scheme adopted much more widely, especially in large or crowded stores. In 1985 Age Concern published a working party report, *The Elderly Shopper*, which examined the position of older consumers. This report clearly showed the desire of older people for such services as seats, toilets and wider aisles in shops, as well as a demand that food—and other goods—be widely available in smaller quantities. What is more, it showed that, in general, the elderly would be willing to pay a little more for such services. Retailers and marketing consultants should be considering these points now and planning better practice for the future.

2. Housing

Moving on from shopping, I would like to discuss the issue of housing, something that is of major importance to older consumers. There are now over 10 million elderly people in the United Kingdom. Taking figures for the United Kingdom as a whole, nearly 48 per cent of households where the head of the household is over the age of 65 years are owner/occupier dwellings, 34 per cent are renting from a council or new town, 3.5 per cent are renting from a housing association and 9.3 per cent rent from private landlords. The Housing Act 1988 has now received royal assent and we can expect major changes in the provision of housing over the next few years. It is too early yet to anticipate exactly what form these changes will take, and how they will affect the older consumer, but there are some very important points that I feel we should consider now. Age Concern in general welcomes any change which is likely to bring an increase in the choice of housing, or any other facility, to the older consumer, but we are anxious to ensure that an adequate standard of housing is available to all older people at a price they can afford. Housing provision at the moment is just not satisfactory. In 1981, out of a total of 6 792 335 households containing at least one pensioner, 55 349 shared a lavatory, 302 958 had no inside lavatory, 751 058 shared a bath, 237 458 had no bath and 173 772 had neither bath nor inside lavatory. This is an appalling state of affairs. All elderly people should have the right to a high standard of accommodation where they can retain their independence and dignity as members of the community. There is an urgent need to provide more accommodation of various kinds designed with the needs and wishes of elderly people in mind, particularly one- and two-bedroom housing, bungalows, and ground-floor and sheltered accommodation. This should be provided across the country and in all housing sectors, particularly through the rented sector and shared ownership schemes where the need is greatest, and growing constantly.

3. Environmental planning

Another area which needs consideration and development is that of environmental planning. We should be developing not only housing, but also other forms of building which blend with existing structures and meet the needs of the people who will be using them, who are typically much older than the families that we have traditionally assumed to be the majority in this country. This applies also to roads, tunnels, crossings, pedestrian precincts, leisure centres and other public facilities which, like homes, should be flexible enough to suit a rapidly ageing population. Many elderly people still need additional help, however, if they are to take advantage of what is or will be on offer in terms of essential services and leisure facilities.

4. Financial help

Age Concern groups around the country take an active role in ensuring that older people are aware of any relevant financial or practical help schemes. They can also offer help and advice with maintenance and general repair. Many groups participate in the Age Concern insurance schemes: one of these policies covers money in gas and electricity meters; another offers cover for home owners who would not otherwise be able to afford to insure their homes against hazards such as burst pipes and fire, but who would find it difficult to pay for the consequences of such damage. Trying to get by on a low income generates many problems for elderly people, and Age Concern is pleased to be able to offer such practical help. We would like to see a much wider variety of services being made availabe to elderly people throughout the country.

5. Health

Health care is another area in which elderly people can be regarded as major consumers, both of National Health Services, and of other complementary services. Age Concern's recent major response to the *Griffiths Report on Community Care* fully stresses the importance of recognizing elderly people as active consumers of health care whose needs and wishes should be considered. We would like to see the development of specially devised programmes in which the needs and desires of the individual could be met by individual 'packages of care', providing a combination of help from the local social services department, the National Health Service and any other appropriate body. The scope for help and care is enormous, and local Age Concern groups offer a variety of services and support to elderly consumers in the form of sitting schemes, visiting schemes, meals on wheels, day centres and other vital help. While primary health care will continue to be provided by the National Health Service, Age Concern believes that the provision of social services—working hand-in-hand with the National Health Service and the care it provides—should be carefully coordinated to ensure the best possible collaboration between statutory authorities, voluntary organizations, private agencies, and families and friends. Community care will be a major facet of health and social service care in the future, and unless we plan to work together we will not be able to ensure that the best possible level of care reaches our elderly customers.

6. Transport

Transport is yet another area in which elderly people can be considered as major consumers. The deregulation of bus services outside the London area has already wrought many changes, and this is an area which is ripe for further development. We have already seen the proliferation of services on popular routes, but the less popular routes, particularly in rural areas, have suffered. Yet there is enormous potential here for the provision and marketing of services. Many consumers, and not only elderly consumers, would willingly support the development of services on these routes and would become regular and reliable users. Age Concern groups provide minibus services in many areas, but they cannot meet all the needs of the local population.

7. Education and leisure

Education and leisure are also important areas for development in the future. As more and more people are retiring early, they will be eager and willing to take advantage of new opportunities. Positive encouragement to elderly people to further their education and to take up new educational and recreational pursuits will enable them to develop new interests and expertise and to participate more fully in community life. There are many different kinds of activity which could be developed and promoted widely—sport, music, dancing, cooking, photography, exercise classes, art and drama, to mention just a few. There is thus a great deal of potential for new activities which has not yet been fully explored.

I hope this brief outline has provided some idea of the sheer range of areas in which elderly people are active consumers. It is very important that they should be recognized as such, and that they are enabled to play a full and active role in society. Old age can no longer be associated with institutions. Older people will have a vital role to play during the next century, including, in many instances, returning to the workforce to meet the gap created by a decreasing number of school leavers. Through my work with Age Concern, I constantly see examples of how rich, happy and fulfilling later life can be. As well as meeting the practical needs of older people, we aim to promote and encourage a more positive view of old age based on independence, choice and self-determination. Older people cannot be happy in a society which does not value them. People working in the fields of planning and marketing could play a vital part by developing strategies and facilities which recognize the value of older consumers in society and explore them as a resource.

References and recommended reading

Abrams, Mark, 'A survey of the elderly shopper', Age Concern, London, 1985
Report of a working party, 'The elderly shopper', ibid., 1985

5
Turning an old problem into a new marketing opportunity
Dr Stephan Buck

Introduction

Marketing requires the collection and interpretation of statistics to suggest who to approach with what goods and services, and how such approaches can best be made.

In this chapter, Stephan Buck adopts this technique to consider the UK market for goods and services among older people. He looks at their general economic position and their spending and saving patterns. This helps to destroy a number of myths about marketing to the old, but leaves the question of how the group can best be approached. To answer this, Stephan Buck examines the media usage of the old, and finally considers how the life histories of people born at different times might affect their attitudes to consumption.

Marketing in general, and advertising in particular, have always been industries dominated by youth, if not in terms of the age of the practitioners, at least in the search for the new and trendy image. In the past this seemed to have the effect of blotting out the old from the consciousness of marketers. Until very recently, perhaps five years ago, this was rationalized on the basis that the old were retired, no longer had an earned income, and therefore were too poor to provide a market for any businesses except a few specialized medicines or cheap foods.

It is questionable whether this view has ever been true; it is quite certain that it has been false since the Second World War and probably since the First World War. Nevertheless, it maintained a grip on marketers for a very long time, in spite of their supposed reliance on the hard facts presented by market research. As we shall see, this in turn is largely explained by the fact that market research, like any other form of science, is only as accurate as the researcher. If astronomers are looking for canals on Mars, that is what their telescopes seem to show them, and the most prized form of telescope will be the one that shows the clearest canals. Similarly, market research can apparently provide evidence supporting a decision to ignore the old, although, for reasons I will explain later, largely because the results are misunderstood.

Within the last few years, this view has been modified, though by no means totally replaced. It is now admitted that a sizeable proportion of old people *are* in possession of considerable resources. However, it is now argued that although they could spend if they wished, the old on the whole do not wish to do so, and are therefore primarily of interest as savers (where their importance has been recognized) but not really in the purchase of goods or services. Once again, market research evidence is provided for this position, and once again it needs examining with considerable care rather than uncritical acceptance.

We have already seen that, numerically, the over-55s account for one-third of the adult population, a significant proportion by any standards. But the market researcher is primarily interested less in the size of a group than in its members' buying power and readiness to buy. Perhaps the most widely used discriminator by market researchers is that of the socio-economic group often called, slightly inaccurately, Class. This is divided into six

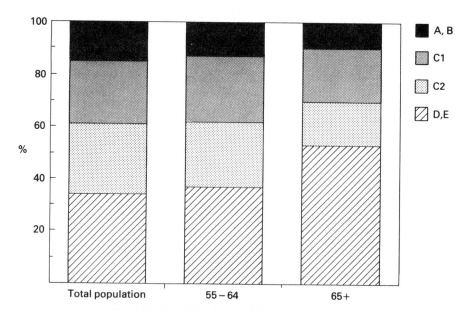

Fig. 5.1 Social class by age (*Source*: AGB, 1989)

categories, A, B, C1, C2, D and E, with desirability from a marketing point of view following the descending order. Class E, at the bottom, consists of people who are poor and do not have an earned income. This has always seemed to marketers to be an accurate description of the old, and helps to explain why they can so easily be ignored. It has already been demonstrated in Chapter 2 that such an assumption is very dubious. For convenience, I repeat the figures given in Fig. 5.1, which show that even among those over 65 years, almost half the population do not come into Classes D, E while among the 55–64 group, the proportion falling into these categories is not very different from that of the population as a whole.

The figures in Fig. 5.1 also make an important point which I will refer to frequently, namely the danger of talking about people over 55 years as one homogeneous group. In this instance, the 55–64 group is very close to the population as a whole, while the over-65s are, if not the complete Class E paupers of popular imagination, at least markedly different in socio-economic grouping from the younger age groups.

There remains another question to be answered. If half of the over-65s do not come into the D, E category, why is this? One possibility would be that a considerable proportion of them are still working, but figures given in Chapter 2 show that this is not the case. Economic activity among the over-65s is low, and has been declining heavily since the early 1970s. Even among the 55–64 age group, a considerable and growing proportion has given up work. So the reason that so many older people do not come into the D, E category is that they are not poor, in other words that they have sources of income apart from the minimum state pension. But what are these sources of wealth?

Figure 5.2 can be regarded as a bird's eye view of economic activities by age. It examines the spending, saving and borrowing patterns of the British population by age group; and the interrelations of these three areas provides a fascinating picture. In all cases, the average for all ages is taken as 100.

The expenditure pattern probably causes least surprise. It is relatively low in the youngest age groups, partly because people of this age may be living with relatives, partly because most have not yet assumed family responsibilities. Expenditures are higher during the 30s and 40s, and then decrease during the 50s, falling still further over the age of 60 years. All this seems very much in line with conventional wisdom. But the other two lines on the chart might well cause more surprise.

Borrowing largely follows the same pattern as spending, but to a very much exaggerated extent. It rises dramatically in between 25 and 50 years, but thereafter falls, equally quickly, to the extent that over-60s borrow less than one-quarter of the all-ages average. Savings, on the other hand, follow an entirely different pattern. They are far below the all-ages average until

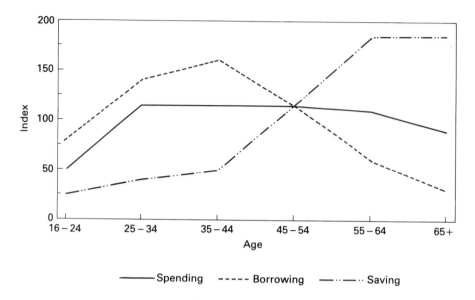

——— Spending   - - - - Borrowing   — ·· — ·· Saving

Fig. 5.2   Spending, borrowing and saving by age (*Source*: AGB index)

the mid-40s, but then begin to increase rapidly. In the 50s they reach the all-ages average (as do the other areas—an interesting coincidence) and then rise steeply so that by the late 50s and 60s savings are close to double the average.

Figure 5.2 makes a very clear point. People below the age of 50 years do indeed spend more than those above, but they often run into debt to do so. Marketers looking for those holding wealth, or indeed available resources, would do well to pay more attention to the older age groups. Over-55s in general account for one-third of the population, but for more than 60 per cent of all savings.

However, the picture is more complicated than this simple statistic would suggest. When in Fig. 5.3 we break down the over-55s by thirds, into high, medium, and low saving categories, we find that the high savers among the old, by definition making up 11 per cent of the population, have 50 per cent of all savings. The bottom one-third of the over-55s, also 11 per cent of the population, have less than 1 per cent of all savings. This is an extremely polarized situation, and it is of particular social and economic significance when it is remembered that relatively few of the over-55 age group have income from employment, but are instead largely dependent on state pensions plus any income from savings. This helps to explain why it is so necessary for both social services and marketers to find ways of distinguishing between, and communicating with, the well-off *and* the poor sectors of the old.

The statistics in Figs 5.2 and 5.3 apply only to relatively short-term savings. They do not cover the ownership of property. However, a very similar picture applies there. Figure 5.4 shows housing tenure by age. Since these statistics come from government sources, the age breaks are not exactly the same as in the earlier statistics, but the picture is clear. More than 40 per cent of the over-60s age group own their houses outright, far more than any other age group. This not only gives them an asset which in most parts of the country has greatly increased in value, but also means that, unlike most younger households, they do not have the burden of mortgage payments. On the other hand, over one-third of the over-60s group lives in council accommodation, again a considerably higher proportion than in younger groups.

This dichotomy may not exactly mirror the one shown in Fig. 5.3, but it would be most surprising if there were not a close relationship. This means that when we look at the over-55s from the point of view of a marketer, we are really looking at two relatively distinct groups, one of which if not entirely fitting the prejudices of those who regard the old as being located somewhere between the poor house and the graveyard, at least can be said to have some similarities to this caricature. But there is another group, who are completely different. It comprises people who are probably better off than they have ever been in their lives, with relatively low outgoings and high and

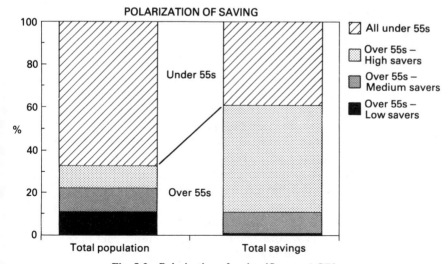

Fig. 5.3 Polarization of saving (*Source*: AGB)

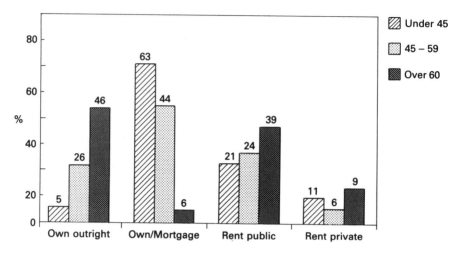

Fig. 5.4   Housing tenure by age of head of household (%) (*Source: OPCS General Household Survey*, 1986)

growing resources. They no longer have children dependent on them; indeed they often receive gifts from their children. They have paid off their mortgages; they are in receipt of pensions, often both state and private, income from investments and quite often bequests from family. By any standards they would appear to constitute a desirable market. But there are two questions to be raised. The first is, are there enough of these high-income groups to be significant and, if so, are they really in the market for buying goods? The second is if they are, how can they be reached? We examine these questions in turn.

Perhaps the most influential figures casting doubt on the readiness of the old to spend money are shown in Table 5.1. These come from the Family Expenditure Survey, and show weekly household expenditures according to the age of the housewife. Even this suggests that the 55–64-year-old household has considerable spending power, but it charts a very rapid decline over the age of 65 years, the 65–74-year-old household spending one-third less than the average, and the household with a head over 75 years spending less than half as much. This covers expenditures on all product areas and seems to support the stereotype of the over-65s living in poverty in a garret. But, as I said earlier, statistics need interpretation, and can very easily be used unthinkingly to support preconceived ideas.

The statistics in Table 5.1 show household expenditure, but the expenditure of a household must be crucially affected by the number of people in that household. Other things being equal, the smaller the household, the less

Table 5.1 Weekly household
expenditure by age of head of household

	Expenditure £	Index
All	189	100
50–64	207	110
65–74	131	69
75+	88	47

Source: FES, 1987

the expenditure. This point is so obvious that it tends to be overlooked, but when we take it into account, the picture shown by Table 5.1 looks very different. Table 5.2 adjusts the earlier figures by household size, and shows that the 65–74-year-old individual spends roughly as much as the all age average, while even the over-75-year-old spends less than 20 per cent below that average, Once again, the reality looks markedly different from the myth.

Although spending by the old is much closer to the average than is usually realized, one must not take this as an indication that the old are no different from others in their spending patterns. Marketers of jeans or pop music do not generally regard the old as being in their market, and they are quite right not to do so. Later, I shall discuss in more detail the product areas which are most favoured by the over-65s; but first we look at the wider picture. Figure 5.5 looks at the 65–74 age group, which spends almost as much per person as the average, and breaks down the expenditure figures by different broad

Table 5.2 Weekly individual expenditure
by age

	Expenditure £	Index
All	74	100
50–64	88	118
65–74	75	101
75+	63	84

Source: FES, 1987

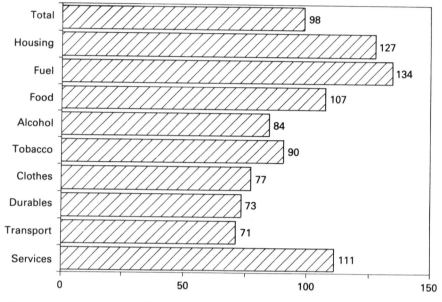

Fig. 5.5   *Per capita* expenditure of the old, compared to the total population (all individuals = 100) (*Source*: FES, 1986)

categories. It can be seen that the areas of highest expenditure are housing, fuel, services and food. The housing figures are deceptive, since mortgage payments do not, for the purposes of the Family Expenditure Survey, count as spending, so the major gain of those older people who own their houses outright is not registered. Perhaps the most surprising piece of information is that the old spend more on food than the average. In fact, once again, these figures underestimate the relative expenditures of the old on buying and preparing food, since the Family Expenditure Survey includes 'eating out' under food expenditure, an area where the old are notoriously low spenders.

This fact is demonstrated in Fig. 5.6, taken from the National Food Survey, which shows expenditures on various food categories by the over-55s compared to the all-ages average. It will come as a considerable surprise to most people to realize that even the over-75s spend more on major food areas such as meat, milk, beverages, etc., than the average; and in many cases, the difference is very significant.

At this point one must insert a word of warning. Marketers of food products tend to think in terms of households rather than individuals, and they have a reason for this. In general one person (the housewife) tends to buy for the entire household, and it is more advantageous for the seller to reach the heavy buyer, which in practice means the person who is purchasing for several people. This is why so much attention has been paid to the relatively young housewife whose family is still at home. One can certainly agree with this line of reasoning. If there is a choice between a housewife buying for several, and a single-person household, it makes commercial sense to deal with the former. Once, that would have been the entire story, but this is no longer the case.

The reason for the change is that the days of mass markets and mass brands are rapidly departing. The name of the game in selling fast-moving consumer goods is now segmentation, tailoring new products to meet the requirements of specific sectors of the market. When this happens, the household is no longer the unit to consider, rather it is the individual. Even when the housewife is buying for several people, one expects that she will buy what suits their individual tastes, and the same is true to an even greater extent when one considers the purchasing patterns of one- or two-person households, particularly those containing people who are not average by reason of their greater age. A combination of the known fact that, individually, older people do spend heavily on some product areas, and the search for greater segmentation, must open up opportunities for marketers to produce fast-moving consumer goods aimed specifically at the older market, as well as financial or other services, where thinking on the part of

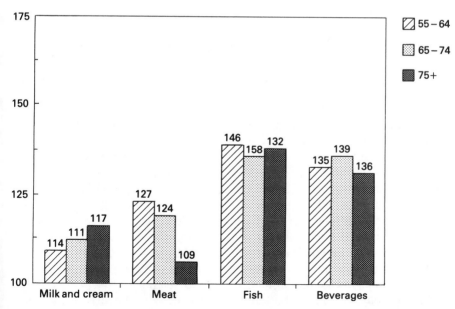

Fig. 5.6 Food expenditures of the old (all adults = 100) (*Source*: NFS, 1987)

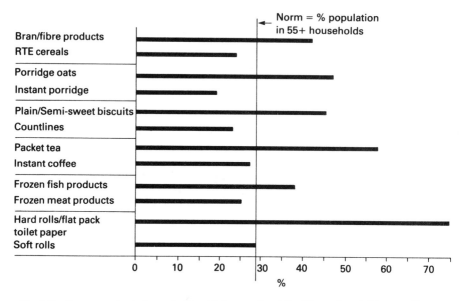

Fig. 5.7   Grocery sales to households with housewives 55+ (% product field expenditure accounted for) (*Source*: AGB, 1988)

producers is rather more advanced. Another chapter looks in more detail at opportunities which have and have not been grasped, and though I do not wish to enter into this area here, it is of interest to use detailed figures from the consumer purchasing panels operated by AGB Research to look at areas where the old buy more than their population share would indicate.

Figure 5.7 contrasts, within certain grocery product areas, those popular with older households as against those preferred by younger people. So the old tend to be heavy consumer of bran products and packet tea, but far less so of ready to eat cereals and tea-bags. The preferences of older people form a rather odd collection, and it is by no means clear that there is any single thread connecting them. However, I suspect that a skilful marketer could draw a number of ideas from this source, especially after a more careful and detailed look at sales patterns and trends. Table 5.3 and Fig. 5.8 do the same for cosmetics and electrical appliances. Again, it must be emphasized that these do not provide all the answers to successful marketing aimed at the old, but at least they should help marketers to ask themselves the right questions.

In examining the marketing habits of the old, it is not enough to know only what they buy, it is also important to know where they buy it. Once again, thanks to consumer panel research, it is possible to produce this kind of

Table 5.3   Cosmetics bought heavily by 55+

	55–64 (%)	65+ (%)
Share of population (female)	14	22
Share of market		
Lip make-up	13	8
Face make-up	14	11
Hair colourants	15	9
Talc	14	14
Yardley	22	35
Bath additives	14	11
Badedas	22	30
Face powder (compressed)	20	27
Max Factor	23	47

Source: AGB

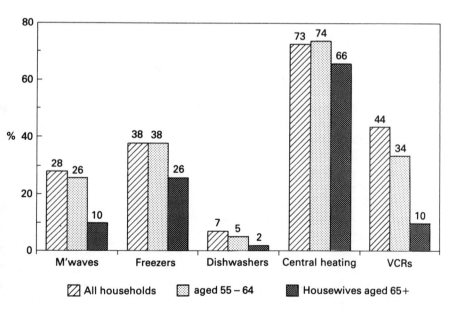

Fig. 5.8   Ownership of some electrical durables (% of households owning) (*Source*: AGB, 1988)

Table 5.4 Visits to grocery stores
by age (% of housewives visiting a
grocery store in a four-week
period)

Age	%
16–24	90
25–34	91
35–44	90
45–64	87
Over-65	85

Source: AGB/TCA

information in considerable detail. The first question is what proportion of the old are capable of undertaking shopping trips? The picture of the housebound old lady being assisted by kind volunteers springs to mind. But as Table 5.4 shows, although such people exist, they are a very small minority, even of the over-65s. In fact, the proportion of older housewives visiting a grocery shop is remarkably close to that of other age groups, 85 per cent compared to 90 per cent for the most active housewife group, 35–44-year-olds.

However, if the propensity of older people to shop is close to that of the average, they tend to have a markedly different pattern in store preference. Figures 5.9 and 5.10 examine the purchasing patterns of the old for grocery items and major electrical appliances. Figure 5.9 shows that the superstores which have proved particularly popular among younger people with cars do not suit the requirements of the old. Proportionally, Asda, the pioneer and one of the leading superstore operators, is visited 29 per cent less by old people than the average. The old are obviously much more likely to buy from local small stores, the Symbol groups and the independents. This is not surprising, but once again makes an important marketing point for organizations intending to aim products at the older market. Similarly, with electrical appliances, the old are particularly loyal to Electricity Boards, and tend not to buy electrical products from multiple stores. These facts contain messages of importance to both retailers and manufacturers of consumer durables.

So far, we have looked at the purchases of goods by the old, but have not considered the service sector, particularly financial services, where, as we have seen (Fig. 5.2) the older age groups are particularly important. It is clear that the old or, to be more precise, a significant section of the old, have the spare resources to dominate the savings market, but there remain two important questions to be answered; first, what are the savings preferences of older people and, second, how can the one-third of the over-55s who control 50 per cent of savings (Fig. 5.3) be distinguished from the remaining two-thirds? Once again, we can only begin to answer these complex questions, but research can provide a great deal of useful information on which answers might be based. Figure 5.11 is relevant to the first of these questions. It looks at the importance of different age groups to different forms of savings. Naturally, it shows that older people are heavy holders of most types of saving, but there are important variations between different savings types and also between the 45–64-year-old group and those over 65 years. The latter, for instance, although holding on average almost twice as much in large building society accounts as all age groups, are still below the 45–64 group in this respect. For government stock and local authority bonds, on the other hand, the over-65s save significantly more than the 45–65-year-old group. The most interesting point in the diagram is that the over-65s in particular save relatively little in unit trusts and equities, which in view of their dominance of the savings market obviously suggests that there remains a considerable public relations task for the equity market in convincing older people that these holdings are not as risky as many apparently believe. With the growing number of privatization issues and increasing competition in the

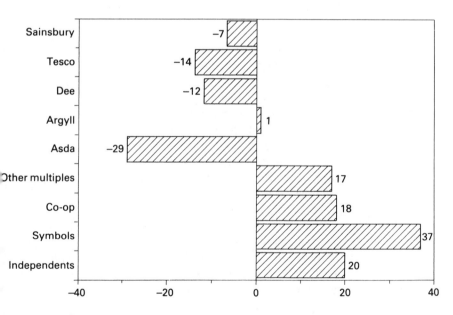

Fig. 5.9 Grocery stores used by housewives 65+ (% difference composed to all housewives) (*Source*: AGB)

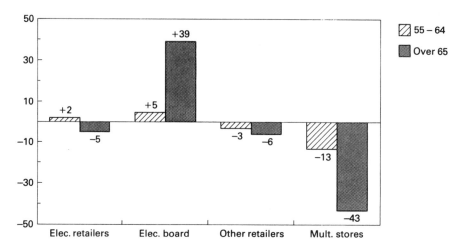

Fig. 5.10 Electrical stores used by 55+ households (% difference compared to all purchasers) (*Source*: AGB)

savings market generally, attempts to attract the large amounts of funds held by older people are likely to become central issues in financial marketing.

To summarize this part of the chapter, we can say that a case has been made for greater selectivity at all levels. The mass markets are generally in decline in every area of spending or saving that one examines. The number of brands of, for instance, grocery products is increasing rapidly, as is the number and variety of savings options. If there was ever a case for ignoring the old on the basis that a considerable proportion of that age group consists of the very poor, such a case no longer holds water, on the equally sound basis that a considerable proportion of the group are also rather rich, and they certainly constitute a market that is sufficiently affluent and numerically large to meet the smaller market sizes at which the more segmented products aim. One of the major developments in marketing theory in recent years has been a growing interest in target marketing, that is to say, developing products and advertising approaches targeted at particular subgroups. The over-55s market, with its considerable degree of polarization, is an obvious example of where such a policy should be applied. But this line of thought is only valid if marketers can make the distinctions they need within the population in general, and the over-55s population in particular. In order to answer that question, the marketer turns to the market researcher for help.

It can be argued that all market research discrimination is designed to produce proxy variables as substitutes for what marketers really want to know. The marketer's objective is to know who is buying his product, who might buy his product and how the former can be kept loyal and the latter persuaded. The market researcher tells him, in very round terms, the sorts of people he appeals to (young rather than old, upper class rather than lower, etc.) and the marketer normally has to make the best of this by approaching the sort of demographic category which he has been told favours the good he is trying to sell. Of course, such a technique works better than nothing, or it would not have been continued for so long, but it has weaknesses, and these are particularly evident when dealing with the old as a group.

By concentrating on the over-55s group, the market researcher is already looking at one particular demographic category, and market researchers often seem to find it difficult to discriminate more finely than this. Even when they do, a situation where there is as much polarization of wealth as is to be found among the old makes accurate selection particularly difficult. I do not believe that any simple demographic can completely answer the problem of selecting that proportion of the old which is of most interest to marketers, but certain standard demographics can be of assistance.

Table 5.5 uses the standard socio-economic breakdown as a guide to those among the old who are heavy savers. Clearly, it is not a bad discriminator, in the sense that those over-65s in Classes D, E have holdings in national savings amounting to about 40 per cent of those in Classes A, B, and building society deposits one-quarter as large.

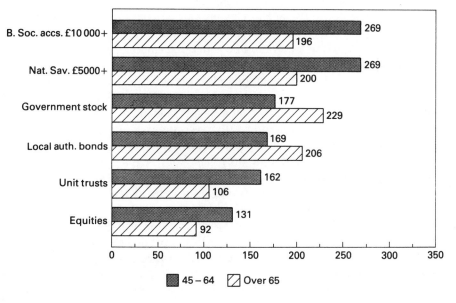

Fig. 5.11   Importance of the old to various types of saving (*Source*: RSGB)

Table 5.5 Saving by 65s+, by class

	Building society deposits		National Savings	
	All	65+	All	65+
All	100	100	100	100
A, B	183	168	183	186
C1	101	104	105	111
C2	75	112	54	76
D, E	55	46	75	70

Source: RSGB

If one can split the over-65s age group by class, one can obviously go a considerable way towards selecting those subgroups of interest to marketers. Nevertheless, it might have been expected that the discrimination by social class amongst the old would have been greater than amongst all age groups but this does not happen to any significant extent. There is a relationship between class and size of savings among the old, but there are also other factors, and a considerable amount of research work done at AGB over the years has shown that heavy savers, particularly among the old, come from all social classes.

The most effective way of linking purchasing or saving habits to exposure to the media is not to use age or class as a proxy, but rather to go directly from the required characteristic (buying my brand, heavy saving, etc.) to use of the media. AGB has experimented with this technique, and has produced a number of valuable insights, but the problem here is that such work is expensive if carried out on a continuous basis and is unsatisfactory if done only occasionally. However, in the work which follows, I show some results of the links that we made between saving and media exposure since, although now some years old, they still have a number of points of interest.

This brings us to the final question facing anyone trying to market goods or services to the old. How can the appropriate group be reached by advertising in the media, and what message should be presented to it? The latter point is of course crucial, but it is dealt with elsewhere in the book, so I will concentrate on the choice of media in marketing to older people.

In practice, a choice of which media to attempt to reach the old selectively comes down to television and the press. Old people do listen to the radio; in fact they are the mainstay of BBC Radio 4 where advertising is not permitted but, unfortunately for the advertiser, they are relatively light listeners to the commercial channel, ILR, whose programme format normally appeals more to the young. To an even greater extent the same is true of the cinema, while posters are a necessarily unselective medium. Television, on the other hand, and particularly Independent Television, is highly popular with older people, and the old are about average in their purchase of newspapers generally, although they have a distinctive pattern of readership, which we shall discuss. But first we look at television.

Television viewing habits lend themselves to analysis by the market researcher. Standard market research variables such as age and class prove to have a high predictive value in judging how much television people watch, and even which channel they prefer. Table 5.6 shows viewing habits of the UK population broken down by age and class. Two facts are obvious at first sight. The lower the class to which a person belongs and the older he is, the more likely he is to watch television. Thus, Classes A, B, the most sought after classes by advertisers, watch almost one-quarter less television than the average. The second obvious fact is that the old in any class watch more than the young in the same class. Thus the over-65 A, Bs watch 17 per cent more television than do the average of all classes. This in fact puts them on a par with Classes D, E as a whole, although still a long way below the over-65s in Classes D, E, who watch 45 per cent more television than the average.

This is good news for the advertisers who are trying to approach the affluent old. One of the problems facing advertisers generally is that members of the most affluent group, Classes A, B, are, as we have seen, light television viewers, which makes them more difficult to approach. But the affluent old are relatively heavy television viewers, which should encourage advertisers in their marketing efforts towards this group. The fact that relatively little television advertising, at least until recently, appears to have been aimed at this group suggests yet more missed opportunities. The advertisers can also take comfort from the channel preference of the old, as is shown in Table 5.7. Not only do the old watch more television, they particularly watch more Independent Television.

Table 5.6   Hours of TV viewing indexed by age and class (all adults = 100)

	All	55–64	65+
A,B	76	88	117
C1	94	112	130
C2	96	116	147
D,E	119	136	145

Source: BARB/AGB, March 1988

Table 5.7 Television viewing
index by channel (all ages = 100)

	Over-55s
all TV	151
BBC1	139
BBC2	157
ITV	163
C4	145

Source: BARB/AGB, March 1988

This is only the start of marketing selectivity. I already pointed out that, for many purposes, the socio-economic categories are good but they are not the perfect discriminators of old people that particular advertisers most want to approach. I shall come to this point shortly. But there are other ways in which advertisers can make their campaigns more cost-effective. To give just two examples, even though they are heavy television viewers, the old are not completely unselective and, in any case, it may well pay advertisers to use those slots which are relatively unpopular with younger people.

Table 5.8 examines the times of the day when over-55s view heavily relative to the rest of the population. It can be seen that, using this criterion, the best times are between 1.00 p.m. and 10.30 p.m. Breakfast television is not so ideal for reaching old people; neither is late night television.

As well as examination of the time of day, one can study individual programme preferences which, although necessarily backward-looking, can be useful for predictive purposes with reference to a series or a particular

Table 5.8 ITV viewing index by
daypart (all adults viewing = 100)

Time	Adults 55+
06.30–09.30	75
09.30–13.00	130
13.00–17.30	151
17.30–22.30	149
22.30–00.00	120
00.00–06.30	100

Source: BARB/AGB, March 1988

Table 5.9   Top 10 Independent Television, and Channel 4 programmes, by television ratings, for over-65s audiences

		Television rating	'000s	Index
1. Coronation Street	ITV	52	4173	159
2. Sporting Triangles	ITV	50	4010	225
3. Emmerdale Farm	ITV	47	3764	201
4. Busman's Holiday	ITV	45	3624	223
5. Murder She Wrote	ITV	41	3311	168
6. Wish You Were Here	ITV	41	3270	161
7. Krypton/Int'l	ITV	39	3147	180
8. Catchphrase/Spel	ITV	39	3103	173
9. Catchphrase	ITV	38	3087	149
10. Headlines	ITV	38	3031	180

Source: AGB Programme Profiles, March 1988

type of programme (e.g. snooker); AGB have a service called *Programme Profiles*, which can rank the preferred viewing of different demographic groups over any weekly or monthly period. There are two ways of doing this, both of value to marketers, but providing different information. Table 5.9 shows those programmes on commercial channels which are watched by the greatest number of over-65s. These are all ITV programmes, and are not very different from the all-adults top 10. Table 5.10, on the other hand,

Table 5.10   Top 10 Independent Television, and Channel 4 programmes, ranked by selectivity index, for over-65s audiences

		Television rating	'000s	Index
1. Mavis on 4	Ch 4	6	447	343
2. International Snooker	Ch 4	17	1347	339
3. Years Ahead	Ch 4	8	669	305
4. South Riding	Ch 4	9	704	298
5. Channel 4 News	Ch 4	4	351	298
6. Weekend World	ITV	5	433	296
7. Channel 4 Racing	Ch 4	7	569	286
8. Fifteen-to-One	Ch 4	25	2036	284
9. Morning Service	ITV	4	341	279
10. News at 12.30	ITV	15	1205	272

Source: AGB Programme Profiles, March 1988

Table 5.11 Readership of national daily newspapers
(all adult readership = 100)

	55–64	65+	A, B social class
Qualities			
Daily Telegraph	121	133	295
The Times	86	61	346
Guardian	79	39	278
Independent	71	39	295
Financial Times	71	33	300
Middle			
Daily Express	114	128	119
Daily Mail	100	111	136
Today	86	39	96
Populars			
Daily Mirror	107	89	34
Sun	79	72	34
Star	79	56	23

Source: National Readership Survey

shows those programmes which have the highest *proportion* of over-65s viewers in their total viewing. Most of these are Channel 4 programmes, and many have relatively low viewing figures in total. It is up to the advertiser to decide which of these approaches is most useful to him, or indeed whether he wants some combination of both, but the important point is that a great deal of information is available which can help marketers to reach selectively the old through television.

In spite of some moves towards greater selectivity, television remains to a considerable extent a mass medium, and few programmes have a viewing profile which is heavily skewed away from the average viewing figures. National newspapers and magazines, on the other hand, tend to be a great deal more selective, particularly by class, but also by age. Table 5.11 looks at national daily newspapers and shows their selectivity by age and class. Clearly, there are major differences. Papers such as the *Daily Telegraph* and the *Daily Express* and *Sunday Express* appeal to both the 55–64 age group, and the over-65s. This can be contrasted with such newspapers as the *Star*, the *Guardian* and the *Financial Times*, which have an extremely young readership profile. It is noticeable that the appeal to a particularly young or old readership does not depend on the class appeal of a newspaper. The table shows the proportion also of Classes A, B readers of national daily newspapers, and it can be seen that the *Star* and the *Sun*, with the lowest, and *The Times* and the *Financial Times*, with the highest, all have relatively young profiles, while the *Daily Telegraph* with a high class profile, the *Daily Express* with a medium one and the *Daily Mirror* with a relatively low profile all appeal to older people. This fact is useful for advertisers, since it allows them to select newspapers which are likely to meet both their age and class criteria. This is not new information to most advertiser. One of the areas in which marketing to the old has been better exploited than most is by savings institutions, using the *Daily Telegraph* and the *Sunday Express* as ways of communicating with the affluent old. But the question is whether there are not many other areas which could equally find these people a worthwhile market.

Magazines are even more selective than newspapers, not least in the age of their readership. Table 5.12 shows a very small selection from the thousands of magazines on the market, biased in favour of those of reasonable size, and with a particular appeal to the old. Some come as no surprise, for instance *Choice*, which is designed for older people, or the *Lady*, which has a somewhat similar image. Others are more surprising, such as *Reader's Digest* or *My Weekly*. Once again, magazines are as selective in terms of class as in terms of age, so many opportunities exist to appeal to the affluent old.

Table 5.12   Magazine readership (all adult readership = 100)

	55–64	65+
Weekly		
TV Times	92	107
Radio Times	100	121
Weekly News	150	171
Garden News	208	186
Amateur Gardening	258	171
People's Friend	146	205
My Weekly	123	153
Woman's Weekly	131	132
The Lady	108	163
Monthly		
Reader's Digest	125	150
Practical Gardening	183	167
BBC Wildlife	125	150
The Field	183	142
Illustrated London News	142	158
Choice	175	267

Source: National Readership Survey, 1987

Table 5.13 Media selectivity of the heavy saver aged over 55 years

	All adults	All over-55s	Heavy savers aged over 55 years
Independent Television	100	125	90
Daily Telegraph	100	107	239
Other quality dailies	100	83	128
Quality Sunday papers	100	84	162

Source: AGB Index, 1983

Earlier, I discussed the problem of converting standard market research data into information about exactly which kind of people a marketer might wish to approach. I also said that the best answer, if it were possible, would be to link the exact characteristic required by the marketer (for instance the fact of being a buyer of a specific brand) with media exposure. I thought it might be helpful to give some evidence of how this works, based on a study carried out by AGB in the mid 1980s which examined the media exposure of committed savers aged over 55 years. Table 5.13 looks at the readership of selected national newspapers and the ITV viewing of committed savers aged over 55 years, and compares them with all adults in the over-55s category and with the population as a whole. It can be seen immediately that committed savers behave in markedly different ways from the over-55 population as a whole, being much more prone to read quality newspapers and significantly lighter viewers of ITV. This can only be seen as a starting point for a more thorough examination of the whole area, but there is enough here to indicate how important such single-source data can be.

The final point is that, for marketers, the world is in a constant state of flux. I have pointed out that in a number of cases the 55–64-year-old universe behaves quite differently from the universe of people aged over 65 years. This must be due in part to their differing work and health circumstances, but is also very likely to be affected by the circumstances of their youth. The person reaching the age of 55 years in the 1980s probably remembers relatively little of the period before the Second World War, and spent his formative years during the War and the period of austerity which followed it. The person reaching 65 years, on the other hand, would have considerable experience and memory of the slump in the 1930s. It would be surprising if these different experiences did not, even after this lapse of time, evoke different spending patterns. This becomes even more relevant when one realizes that before long, during the 1990s, people whose formative years were spent in the more consumer-orientated 1950s will reach the age of 55 years. This point is considered in greater detail in a later chapter.

The target for any marketer tends to move rapidly, a fact that has long been realized about the young, but is equally true of the old. The only certainty is that for a very long time to come this target will be increasingly affluent and worth making an effort to reach. It will be fascinating to see how effectively marketers deal with the challenge.

References and recommended reading

Admap, 'Over 50s: gold amongst the grey', seminar proceedings, London, 25 October, 1989

Broadcasters Audience Research Board, weekly 'Television Audience Reports', London

Day, E., B. Davies, R. Dove, W. A. French, 'Reaching the senior citizen market(s)', *Journal of Advertising Research* (USA), December 1987/January 1988

Economist Conference Unit, 'The ageing population: the new growth market', proceedings of conference at The Hilton, London, April 1987

Esomar, 'The untapped goldmine: the growing importance of the over-50s', Paris conference, book of conference papers, Amsterdam, 15–17 March 1989

French, W. A. and R. Fox, 'Segmenting the senior citizen market', *Journal of Consumer Marketing*, 2, 1 (1985), pp. 61–74, USA

HMSO, Central Statistical Office, *Family Expenditure Survey*, London

Ibid., Office of Population Censuses and Surveys, *General Household Survey*, London

Ibid., Ministry of Agriculture, Fisheries and Food, *National Food Survey*, London

Joint Industry Committee for National Readership Surveys, *National Readership Survey*, London

Langer, J., 'The elderly market: selected readings', American Marketing Association Publications Division, New York, 1982

Lumpkin, J. R. and T. A. Festervand, 'Purchase information sources of the Elderly', *Journal of Advertising Research* (USA), December 1987/January 1988

Schewe, C. D. (ed.), 'Consumers in transition: in-depth investigations of changing lifestyes', AMA management briefing, American Marketing Association Publications Divison, New York, 1985

Uncles, M. D. and Ehrenberg, A. S. C., 'Brand choice among older consumers', working paper, London Business School, 1989

6
Opportunities, grasped and ungrasped
John Gabriel

Introduction

It is becoming more widely accepted that marketers have underestimated the old, but there remains the question of the best areas to exploit. John Gabriel looks at a number of cases where firms have recognized the potential of the ageing population and, as a result, have created highly successful businesses. He also considers areas where opportunities have been missed, and looks at the kind of marketing approach which would help companies to take advantage of the increasingly important market offered by older people.

In any discussion of marketing, generalizations are easy to make and exceptions to them even easier to find. It is one of the major themes of this book that there is a variety of opportunities for marketing to the older age groups which is not being grasped effectively at present due to limited vision on the part of the marketers. However, although this is undoubtedly true, we must note equally the many areas in which successful markets have been developed while relying primarily on Third Age consumers.

In this chapter we cover areas such as financial services, holidays, magazine publishing and pharmaceuticals, which have all shown marked successes in building profitable businesses on sales to the older consumer. This is only a small selection from the much greater number of similar businesses. Nevertheless, it is also fair to say that such cases remain the exception rather than the rule. Of course, in many areas, there would be no point in trying to create a market among older people. But, as we have shown in earlier chapters, in view of the number of Third Agers in the community, and the wealth at their disposal, it may well be argued that efforts so far have done little more than touch the surface of the enormous potential market. This is particularly the case in the large fields of selling fast-moving consumer goods and durables. It is believed that in both these areas more attention is now being paid to the potential of the old, but it is difficult to persuade firms to provide material for case studies because they do not wish to reveal the secrets of their success, or of their failure.

From those cases which we were able to examine, two main points emerged as being common to success in selling to older age groups. The operations which work have incorporated a deep understanding of the requirements, motivations and aspirations of older people. They also incorporate communication with the elderly in ways that treat them as normal, responsible adults rather than as an unfortunate subspecies of humanity, divorced from the real world of the consumer. In many areas companies which adopt such an approach reap considerable benefits. The fascinating questions for marketers are how many more areas would be conducive to similar marketing techniques, and who will be the first companies to produce the brands which achieve success?

1. The Saga saga

There is one company whose name has become synonymous with older people and that is Saga. A 'Saga holiday' is widely interpreted as a group of older people going somewhere together, at a very competitive price, probably in the off-season (Fig. 6.1). What is the story behind this success? How has it been achieved?

It all began in 1949 when Folkestone hotelier Sidney De Haan was trying to think up ways of filling his hotel outside the then normal holiday months of June–September. He realized that the only people who were free to holiday outside the season were pensioners, but they had very little money. (A state pension then was about £1.30 per week.) He put an advertisement in a Bradford newspaper offering a week's holiday with travel, meals en route, full board and three excursions, all for £6.50. He was overwhelmed with responses, filled his own hotel and several others to accommodate the overflow.

This was just the beginning. Within a few years spring and autumn saw pensioners flocking to south coast resorts in such numbers that De Haan was able to negotiate with British Rail to charter special trains to bring them south. (This link grew to such an extent that Saga at one stage accounted for over half a million train journeys a year.)

Another initiative was taken in 1959 when De Haan was able to convince both the UK and French governments to allow no-passport day trips. With flights between Lydd and Le Touquet, hundreds of UK trippers gained their first taste of France, and French trippers of the United Kingdom. From here the initiative moved to the sunny coasts of the Mediterranean. By using the spare capacity of both airlines and hotels in the 'off-peak', Saga has been able to negotiate extremely good deals. These have benefited the airlines

Fig. 6.1   Saga holiday brochures covers

and the hotels by providing them with business in their quiet periods. They
have also enabled Saga to offer very good value packages to their customers.
Because the 'season' varies from country to country, it is now possible to
take a Saga holiday at any time of the year somewhere in the world. The
growth in destinations, and the changes in customer requirements, is
reflected in the range of 10 brochures now on offer, compared to two only
nine years ago (one overseas and one local). This also reflects the current
Saga holiday takers who in their younger years were among the pioneers of
the early package tours in the 1950s. They are seasoned travellers who know
their way around and can cope in the countries they visit. They have done the
milk runs and now want something different, something more unusual. Saga
caters for them with packages such as Kenyan safaris or Himalayan treks. In
fact the current options available range from £58 for a week in a comfortable
private hotel in Scarborough on half-board, to about £15 000 for a luxury
round-the-world cruise. Between these limits, there are over 100 centres
abroad and some 65 UK resorts.

Another trend that has developed over the past five years, and that is now
being provided for, is a demand by some for a move away from full-board,

highly organized holidays. Customers now want less rigid packages and like to have at least one meal a day out at a local restaurant.

Saga have always advocated, and practised, a policy of extending a helping hand. They leave as little as possible to chance and provide such things as insurance for the holiday and medical cover as part of the cost. Couriers are on call throughout the journeys and, until recently, the Saga switchboard was manned in the evenings and at weekends to allow customers to phone at cheap rates. This has now been made unnecessary by Saga no longer using travel agents but taking all bookings, queries, etc., on freephone telephone numbers.

The whole holiday business is changing, as are the requirements of older people. Saga is not only keeping abreast with the holiday requirements of their customers, but is continuing to trailblaze new holiday destinations and formats, both within the United Kingdom and abroad.

As another result of their extensive experience in serving retired people, and thus their understanding of them, Saga has come to realize that many of the specific non-holiday-related needs and wishes of these people have not been fulfilled. In order to meet some of these, Saga has expanded its operations to include such areas as a retirement health plan, personal accident, home and car insurance schemes, a funeral prepayment plan, savings schemes and a med+ card. (This latter is a small plastic card which carries the owner's medical details on microfilm so that, should an emergency arise, doctors will be able to administer immediate aid.)

In line with this is the remarkable growth of the Saga magazine. Its popularity has been such that within a four-year period it has progressed from being published quarterly, on a predominantly subscription basis, to 10 instalments per year with a trial on the bookstalls.

This has lead to changes within Saga, with the public company now being called Saga Group plc having three main divisions: Saga Holidays, Saga Publishing and Saga Services. This restructuring is being matched by expansion of management and marketing resources for a group convinced that their future in serving older people is a growing and golden one.

2. The National Savings story

2.1 The thesis

Rewards await those organizations which project themselves in a sensitive and positive way to Third Agers.

National Savings, as a result of getting under the skin of their Third Age audience, were able to communicate more effectively and more successfully than many other organizations. Third Agers wish to be portrayed as the ordinary people that they are—with emotions, hopes and aspirations—just like everybody else. Largely, Third Agers believe, the media has ignored them completely or, worse still, has portrayed them as decrepit or objects of fun. This naïve and damaging view of Third Agers must change if modern marketeers are to cater successfully for the demands of this growing and important section of society (one-third of the adult population, accounting for 40 per cent of the nation's wealth).

2.2 The background to the National Savings story
National Savings have been around since 1861 and hold in the region of £37 billion of the nation's savings. National Savings have a variety of savings products, each of which has a particular appeal to a particular audience. One of these products, the Investment Account, has been mainly targeted at non-taxpayers since 1985, when the composite rate tax was introduced. National Savings products were deliberately exempted from composite rate, so that non-taxpayers would have a savings option where they could receive their interest in full without tax deductions. (Local banks and building societies have to deduct tax from interest and this cannot be reclaimed by a non-taxpayer.)

2.3 Selling the Investment Account
Non-taxpayers, the obvious target group, consist mainly of children and non-working or retired Third Agers. Given the greater savings need of the Third Agers, the advertising was primarily directed at this older audience. The rational proposition was strong: 'local banks and building societies have to deduct tax from the interest you receive on your savings and you cannot claim it back. The National Savings Investment Account takes nothing off for tax—so you receive all the interest in full. If you are a non-taxpayer you are better off with the Investment Account.' This is a complex message —still further complicated by the fact that income from the account itself counts towards your total income and can push you into a tax paying bracket! The message was therefore backed up with a detailed booklet explaining the tax situation and how it can affect savings income.

2.4 We got it wrong before we got it right
The first attempt was a television commercial which employed the analogy of a ball knocking over skittles in a 10-pin bowling alley, a very rational explanation of the benefits showing the symbolic 'tax ball' knocking over a proportion of the 'interest pins'. Results were acceptable but unspectacular. Further consumer research was thus undertaken.

2.5 Researching the Third Agers' motivations: 'getting under their skin'
As with all advertising, unless the consumer is captivated by the commercial,

the message will fall on deaf ears. Our Third Agers were not sufficiently motivated by a rational proposition alone. They wanted to know what the 'end benefit' of saving with such an account would be. They were primarily interested in what they could *do* with the extra interest received as a result of nothing being deducted for tax.

2.6 An advertising 'end benefit'

This led to the line: 'Give your savings a new lease of life.' Understanding our consumers' positive aspirations to enjoy life to the full, led us to Myrtle.

2.7 Dramatizing the benefit through an active lifestyle

Myrtle, in real life, campaigns for a more outward looking and active approach to life for Third Agers. The campaign features Third Agers enjoying an active life to the full: on a fast motorbike, windsurfing and perhaps most famous of all, on a hang glider! To balance these very active television scenarios, we also shot much simpler stories: 'walking along a beach', 'walking the dog' and a 'chance meeting' between a man and a

Fig. 6.2   'Myrtle' hang-gliding

woman. Not only did we take care to show our Third Ager in an active way, we cleverly used a younger non-taxpayer enjoying their company. The relationship between the young and old is very special and gave a chance to show the warmth as well as the fun side of the Third Ager's character.

2.8 Success through understanding
The campaign was hugely successful: 75 per cent prompted awareness of the advertising, a dramatic improvement in the understanding of the message, and 100 000 new accounts opened in one month (March 1987).

2.9 The lessons learnt
Do not ignore Third Agers. They are an increasingly influential group. Do not leave them out of commercials—as we first did. Portray them as they wish to be seen—as active, real people leading full lives. Spell out the product benefit in emotional as well as rational terms. They want to be respected in the community and even those less active non-taxpayers aspire to the imagery developed for National Savings.

3. Avid readers

It is not always necessary to be the inventor or creator of an idea to be able to make it work well. A good example of this exists in the area of publishing for older readers. The Emap group has, over the past five years, acquired two publications: *Choice* and *Yours*, which were started by others and positioned to fulfil different, but complementary, needs.

Choice was started by the Pre-Retirement Association in 1971 and went through some tough years before being bought into the Emap stable. Its prime target market is seen as being those in their immediate pre- or post-retirement years as the editorial content centres on matters relating to money, the home, health and leisure. The readership profile is predominantly composed of Classes A, B and C1 and it is claimed to be 'the cream of the over-55s market'.

Because of the wide range of options, particularly financial, open to older people, no direct links with any supplying companies have been forged. This stance allows *Choice* to 'try to be as independent as we can', and to comment impartially on what is on offer. The basic stance of this monthly magazine is one of providing information rather than providing a vehicle for talking back to the readers.

A spin-off that has developed from the magazine is the *Choice Retirement Briefing File*. This loose-leaf document provides a wide range of information for those newly retired or about to retire. The topics range from new lifestyles and money, to family and friends and caring for older relatives. The

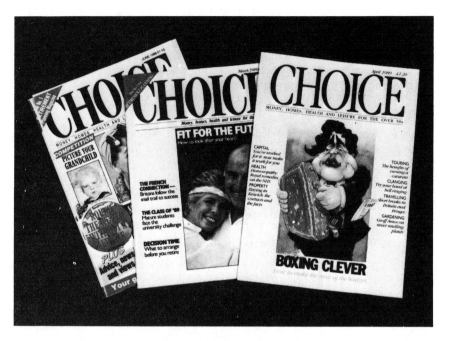

Fig. 6.3   *Choice* magazine covers

file is usually bought by employers to give to employees who are due to retire soon. The client list looks like an investor's dream of blue-chip companies with copies being provided for all from the sweeper to the board. It is not only the large companies who buy, although they do tend to be the most aware of what is involved at retirement.

There are also a number of retirement books that have been published under the *Choice* name as a part of what is, in effect, a retirement library.

The other publication, the monthly newspaper *Yours*, was bought by Emap because it liked what it had seen. The positioning of *Yours* is very different to that of *Choice*. It was originally published on behalf of Help The Aged, largely as a paper to campaign on behalf of pensioners and to put across to pensioners what their rights were. Its current reader profile reflects this as it is more into the Class C2/D,E end of the spectrum. The average age of the readers is the late-60s and upwards, people who are well into their retirement.The paper has much more of a newspaper style and format and aims to be 'a friend to the older person'. It contains more in the areas of entertainment and nostalgia than in the provision of information and advice.

There is a phenomenal response to competitions and letters in the paper, with very strong reader loyalty. This latter is doubtless helped by the fact that the distribution of nearly half of the 130 000 plus copies is carried out by voluntary distributors. This dates back to the days when the paper was published by Help The Aged, with many of the distributors having continued under the new management.

It has, however, not all been plain sailing. There has been the launch, and demise, of a magazine called *Residential Care*, aimed at the management of residential homes for the elderly, and the brief test marketing of *Grandparents*.

Not deterred by this, Emap is planning to optimize its two existing titles and is investigating other areas of the market among the over-55s.

Comment

By acquiring these two publications, Emap has been able to bracket both the more, and less affluent ends of the over-55s market. Keeping close editorial links with both the Pre-Retirement Association and Help The Aged must also have enhanced its credibility.

4. Oiling the joints

Seven Seas Health Care Ltd has been in the business of providing a wide, and expanding, range of products for human health care for over 50 years (Fig. 6.4).

Fig. 6.4   Seven Seas Cod Liver Oil products

As part of its ongoing monitoring of the health care market, Seven Seas Health Care Ltd observed a change in attitudes to health from the 1970s into the 1980s. In the early part of the 1970s, the main concern with health related to those who were ill seeking remedies, with the responsibility for this being handed over to doctors. Since the later part of the 1970s, the trend has been for a greater proportion of the population to take on the responsibility for their own health. The attitude is: 'I am fit and want to stay that way.' One of the specific aids to this, apart from diet, exercise and reduced stress, is an awareness that there are a number of products that one can take to maintain one's health, specifically vitamin, mineral and dietary supplements.

The general level of interest in health matters is relatively low up to the age of about 30 years. It shows an increase up to 40 years and increases markedly thereafter, especially among women. This concern is not limited to Classes A, B, and C1.

One of the areas where the frailty of the human body makes itself felt is in the joints and muscles. Analysis shows that half the population aged over 55 years suffers from arthritis or rheumatism. There is no cure for this, but there are drugs that can help to relieve the pain, although these must be taken for the rest of one's life. As can be imagined, there is a marked reluctance to become dependent on drugs, not to mention the high cost of them. People are, however, happier to take a natural product such as cod liver oil, which has a wide range of anti-inflammatory properties and a good clinical pedigree. With a well-known and established brand of cod liver oil in its range, Seven Seas Cod Liver Oil, the company decided to concentrate its marketing efforts in the elderly market, those aged over 55. Much preparatory work had to be done prior to commitment to a communications programme. This included:

4.1 Brand name

It became apparent from qualitative research that if the brand was not perceived as being 'right' there would be no chance of capturing and holding this market. It must not be seen as too medical, too folksy or too young.

The consumers wanted reassurance on the quality of the product. It had to be of high quality and not necessarily cheap, especially as health is not seen as something one tries to buy on the cheap.

Initial research proved positive. Results were confirmed by a twice yearly tracking study into brand and product perceptions.

4.2 Channels of distribution

It was considered essential that the product be readily available in the places where the over-55s shop. In addition to the conventional outlets the product was also made available via mail order.

Effective point-of-sale material was also perceived as being important. This carried through the main theme of the advertising as well as answering the questions: 'what is it?', 'what does it do?' and 'how do I take it?'. Clear literature was also made available, with the typesizes being large enough to be read easily.

4.3 Communications

As the over-55s are big media consumers, especially of television and the printed word, a campaign had to be developed that would be synergetic in all media.

There are legal restrictions on the claims that can be made in terms of the medical benefits, with cod liver oil, although rich in vitamins A and D, being restricted to 'helps to relieve muscular aches and pains'. The creative campaign that was finally accepted centres on a Wizard of Oz type of character, a Tin Man who was getting on in years and beginning to suffer from aches, pains and stiffness, complaints much relieved after taking Seven Seas.

This campaign, along with three or four others in the early stages, was tested extensively in discussion groups of target customers. From these it was possible to adjust and fine-tune the advertisements. It also confirmed that advertisements were not seen as being too jocular (arthritis is not in joke to those who suffer from it), to be talking down its audience, nor was the wrong style of language being used. It was also researched among some younger groups who, although a little mystified, were not worried or upset by it.

4.4 Media

The advertising agency was requested to provide a detailed analysis of the media usage of the over-55s. Initially, this task seemed to fill the agency with a certain amount of trepidation, since there is little media data for that age group, but its enthusiasm increased markedly as advertising progressed. The agency was also delighted by the opportunities it unearthed, and by the excellent packages it was able to negotiate.

4.5 Packaging

One complaint that had been levelled at the product, in research groups, was that the bottle was difficult to open. The small cap fitted very tightly and was very hard to grip, especially with arthritic hands. The problem was discussed and Seven Seas engineers designed a larger, pentagonal cap that could be turned by pressure from the palm of the hand. This was approved by the Arthritis Association.

4.6 Public relations

The company accepted that the impact of media advertising is limited and needs to be supported. To this end an ongoing PR campaign was carried out in a wide range of publications. In addition, stands have been taken at exhibitions for health visitors. This allows the company to talk to the health professionals who actually visit the elderly, especially those aged 80 years and over, who are the prime sufferers from arthritis. Considerable attention is also paid to getting information through to pharmacy assistants.

All the above is supported by employing within the sales and marketing department a doctor of nutrition who is available at the end of the telephone to answer questions. It is also a policy of the department that all questions and letters be answered on the day that they are received.

How successful has the campaign been? Since the decision to concentrate on the over-55s was implemented, sales have more than doubled. The Tin Man campaign has been running for over a year and is felt to be working well. It will be continued and developed and updated as necessary.

Comment
Here is a company that has investigated its existing markets carefully and found substantial opportunity. It has not been in a hurry but has developed and implemented a comprehensive strategy which is now working; and, given the company's propensity for research, should evolve as time passes, and continue to be profitable.

5. Ungrasped opportunities

As has been demonstrated in the preceding case histories, a number of companies are coming to terms with the opportunities offered by the increasingly affluent older population. They are, however, very much in a minority.

Apart from a lack of knowledge of the proportions of markets accounted for by older people, there is the problem of their invisibility. This invisibility ensures that the old are generally overlooked and it appears to have two root causes. The first is that the old are inconspicuous. The young are obvious by their aural and visual loudness and the very old by their grey hair and physical frailness. It is those aged 50–75 years who are the least noticed. Try yourself to put an accurate age to people walking about in the High Street and see how difficult it is. The second root cause is the age of marketing management. These people are usually the instigators of marketing and advertising strategy and are themselves rarely beyond their mid-40s. Consequently, they empathize much more instinctively with the 16–45-year-olds rather than with an age group of which they have no direct life experience.

This whole situation is worse in advertising agencies where the creatives are likely to be even younger.

Obviously, there are numerous ungrasped opportunities for products and services for the elderly. Some of these fall into the area of designing new products or adapting existing ones which meet the needs specifically, and exclusively, of older people. Others involve a realization that older people are already significant consumers and can be target marketed.

What we attempt to do in this section is to provide some indicators to areas that we feel may well offer opportunities. Inevitably, these will only scratch the surface of what is available but will, hopefully, serve as thought stimulators. We examine them in broad categories.

6. Financial services

Several financial institutions would claim that they are already providing a good range of products for the elderly. Perhaps they feel that they are, but our research has shown that general perceptions of what is on offer are that older people are not being catered for.

Our research has highlighted even more what is perceived as a lack of understanding of, and sympathy for, the needs of older people, many of whom do not like discussing their financial affairs at a desk in a crowded banking hall with a pretty woman in her early 20s. They would prefer both a little more discretion and overt maturity. They also, in common with many younger people, do not wish to feel that what they are being offered is just the standard package. Each person is an individual and wants to be treated as such rather than as a number or, even worse, as a nuisance.

With the increased, and increasing, numbers of women in the workforce, a whole new field of opportunity could be opening up in retirement planning. These are women who have control of their own finances and wish to retain control into their retirement.

Financial needs are markedly different at different stages of the Third Age. Many, especially those at the younger end, may well have substantial sums of cash on several occasions during their Third Age. These occasions can include: the sale of a four-bedroom family home and purchase of a smaller, more appropriate, home; receipt of a lump sum on retirement; the maturity of insurance policies at about 65 years which had been taken out when in their 30s and 40s to provide a little nest egg on retirement; inheritance of property from parents; and life assurance for widows. The needs are likely to be different on each occasion, yet no organization appears to have taken this on board. For example, who offers advice to a new widow? Here is someone whose husband has probably taken care of all household accounts for the past 30 or 40 years and who is now, perhaps for the first time be very frightening and a knowledgeable and sympathetic advisor would be much appreciated.

What about those who are asset-rich, living in valuable properties, but are income-poor and suffering in the basic quality of their lives? They don't know about capital release schemes nor, often, where to turn for impartial advice.

There are also many who are ignorant about such financial matters as their wills and funerals. How many actually claim all the state benefits to which they are entitled, or even know where to go to find out? There must be substantial opportunities to provide valuable and useful products and services within this very broad category.

7. Retailing

A recent publication from Age Concern England entitled *The Elderly Shopper* concluded, *inter alia*, that: 'All those involved in creating shopping centres and shopping environments should be aware that shopping is a leisure activity and should be a pleasurable experience. The environment should reflect this. There should be spaces allowed for people to sit, to talk, to relax and feel safe from threat.'

How appealing are shops and especially chain stores? Why is it, for example, that older people are more inclined to buy their electrical appliances from Electricity Board showrooms than from the High Street discounters? Could it be that the age of the staff is higher, or that the background music is less strident and more attuned to the customers than to the staff? Perhaps these older staff have a more practical understanding of household products rather than the audio/hi-fi/television ranges. Providing a more attractive environment need not only mean chairs and cups of tea.

Very few retailers of any sort seem to have realized, let alone acted upon, the fact that retired people are not restricted in the days of the week on which they can shop. Surely many things can be done to attract them into shops between Monday and Friday in order to boost sales on these relatively quieter days.

Many older people are very discerning shoppers and do not always aim for the cheapest products but, rather, opt for those that provide them with what they perceive to be good value. In order to choose these products they often want more information about the competing brands, either from point-of-sale displays or from the sales staff. Both these are frequently lacking.

Supermarkets are frequently criticized, not only by the elderly, but also by younger people who live in one- or two-person households, for forcing multipacks or large-size purchases. There is a feeling that the buyer of small quantities is being penalized. Portion packs of, for example, chops where in her life, faced with a rates bill and just does not know what to do. This can there is one large and one small chop also come in for criticism, especially from the partner who gets the small chop. Age Concern concluded that 'self-selection of loose fruit and vegetables is welcome and should be used more widely'. Assistance in carrying goods to cars or public transport would also be appreciated.

Another opportunity area must surely be in the area of ladies' fashions. Frequent criticism is heard of fashions all being designed for the young with the mature being ignored. For a considerable number of women this is extremely frustrating. They feel that now, in their retirement years, they have more time available to choose clothes and, in a number of cases, more money to spend on them. Yet they can't find clothes that they like, nor that they feel are suitable. There is also the problem of fit as their figures begin to change with advancing age. As Age Concern comment: 'Generally clothing and footwear products should be designed so as to combine the special needs of elderly people with smart appearance. Multiple stores should stock a wider range of clothing and footwear.'

What about direct mail or the catalogue shops? These forms of retailing could well offer potential, especially in allowing selection to be done in the comfort of one's home. Are the ranges on offer broad enough to appeal to the older householders as well as to the younger nest-builders?

8. Electrical appliances

There appears to exist an attitude in the minds of many that older people don't buy electrical appliances. An inspection of the sales and ownership levels from sources such as AGB's Home Audit Panel show that this is not the case. Despite lack of any real marketing effort directed towards the older population, they are significant buyers in a number of electrical product areas. With over 40 per cent of heads of households aged over 55 years, and with many of these people moving house each year, it should be possible to increase still further with the appropriate marketing effort the sales opportunities in the older segment of the population. Many appliances, such as microwave ovens, are ideal for the one- or two-person household, whether its head is aged 28 or 78 years. Similarly, the smaller, working surface dishwasher is ideal for the small household but is very rarely promoted either by the manufacturers or by retailers.

There is a currently accepted truism that old people do not understand electronic products and suffer from acute technophobia. While there are grains of truth in this in terms of the more sophisticated products such as home computers and, to a much lesser degree, video cassette recorders, it is by no means universal. The acceptance level of microwave ovens is generally close to national levels, especially among the 55–64-year-olds. The results achieved with these appliances are such that they are now seen as an integral part of both the kitchen and of the cooking process.

9. Personal products

It is becoming apparent that there is a growing feeling among retired people that the care of their health lies not only in the hands of the National Health Service, but also in their own. This is manifested by an awareness of the need to take appropriate exercise and of eating correctly as part of their health maintenance regimen. For many, dietary supplements take the form of vitamins or products such as cod liver oil or even ginseng. The awareness of dietary needs is stronger among women, who take the greatest amounts of pills. However, the smaller numbers of men who currently take these products indicates that the creation of a greater level of awareness of their benefits could dramatically increase the size of the market.

Within this broad category are products that can be developed especially for the old, particularly those whose physical powers are beginning to wane. Products designed to make ordinary tasks easier for the less mobile are likely to appeal not only to the elderly but quite probably to the middle-aged too. The Design Centre in London has featured such products, as did an exhibition of Design for Independent Living sponsored by the Museum of Modern Art in New York. The sorts of products that have been featured have included shower seats, hearing aids, lightweight wheel chairs, a portable electronic magnifying device, large key pads/displays for telephones and remote controls for television.

10. Leisure

With retired people now having seven days each week to fill, the need for good leisure products and services is self-evident.

One of the most popular pastimes is gardening, as evidenced by the proportions of gardening products bought by this age group. There is, however, often a change in emphasis in the style of gardening as people get older. There is a tendency to develop and design gardens which reduce the amount of heavy manual labour such as perennials rather than annuals. This has implications in terms of the types of gardening tools required and plants purchased.

On retirement, many people turn to creative hobbies. Some take up painting, usually watercolour, while others embroider or crochet. For a number of men who have spent their main working life in an office environment, retirement opens up a range of opportunities to do things with their hands. For some this means such activities as restoring furniture, while for others it may be bookbinding, making puppet theatres or some other type of craft. The majority of these people need some tuition, be it in the form of books, magazines, part works, adult education courses or videos. They also need the appropriate equipment and supplies.

Many people wish to travel during their Third Age. Obviously, there are many companies, such as Saga, which specialize in the provision of a wide range of holidays or travel opportunities for older people. Regardless of this, the market has by no means reached saturation point and there are numerous opportunities in such areas as special interest groups and local short trips. These latter are particularly appropriate for people who are uncomfortable when away from their homes for more than a night or two. The venues may be local sights or even big shopping centres such as Milton Keynes.

For those who own caravans, touring is obviously possible out of the peak school holiday periods and the owners of caravan sites would do well to promote them more. The possibility of organizing round trips to a number of interesting places, all centred round pre-booked caravan sites, could provide further opportunities.

Another area which does not seem to have been exploited to any significant extent is the depth and range of business and work experience of retired people, not to mention their eagerness to share it. There are continued complaints of shortages of skilled manpower in many fields. Surely some of these could be met by part-time use of retired people; and for an organization to be able to offer a pool of such skills could prove profitable for all concerned.

11. Fast-moving consumer goods

It is easy to overlook the whole area of fast-moving consumer goods, but it is risky to so. In many product fields, the over-55s are the most important consumers, and there are very few products where the elderly have little real impact. For example, the fact that they account for nearly 60 per cent of all packet tea sales, yet only just over one-quarter of instant coffee sales, presents some interesting challenges to tea and coffee marketers.

There are dangers inherent in looking only at product groups sales rather than going down to brand level. In the area of bath additive sales, where women aged over 55 years account for 25 per cent of all sales, they also account for one-half of the sales of one particular brand. To have made assumptions based on the broad 25 per cent figure could have led to incorrect, and expensive, conclusions.

Comment from Rena Bartos on the US situation may well be an indication of developments here.

This awareness of changing consumer needs is manifested in the cosmetics industry as well. Skin care sells well. As the cosmetics consumer grows older she becomes more concerned with the condition of her skin than the latest shade of makeup. One major cosmetics house redesigned its makeup line, adding skin care ingredients to foundations, eye shadows and lipsticks. Other cosmetics makers are offering lipsticks that counteract dryness and face powder that protects against sun damage and skin irritation.

12. Media

There are a small number of publications, such as *Saga*, *Choice* and *Yours*, that are targeted specifically at older people. The range of topics covered tends to be age-specific and certainly gives the impression that there must be scope for more general and in some areas, more interest-specific publications. In America, the magazine *50 Plus* has recently changed its title to *New Choices*, while a new entrant, *Lears*, is designed for 'the woman who wasn't born yesterday'. Both are interesting developments in this burgeoning area.

On television, Channel 4's *Years Ahead* is also targeted at this age group and appears to be being well watched by many for whom it was created. Where television is particularly seen to fall down is in terms of the way it treats older people, or rather fails to treat them. There are regular complaints that most of the fiction on television ignores older people. They are simply not included, although in real life they would have been there. When they are included they tend to be portrayed either as figures of fun or of pity: either Alf Garnett or hypothermia. However, they do not want to be singled out with age-specific labels.

The fact that older people are dedicated television watchers would have made one think that the Independent Television companies would be proud of the numbers of older viewers that they attract. Not a bit of it. For most, the old have to be brushed under the carpet or perhaps apologized for. Surely the purchasing power of older people should be seen as an opportunity to sell television advertising.

13. Conclusion

The preceding comments merely touch on some areas where marketing to the ageing population should be investigated.

For most organizations, the probable starting point is to undertake, or commission, a Third Age audit that will allow them to see exactly where they currently stand *vis-à-vis* the over-55s in their markets. This will allow them to grasp the importance of these people and to assess what strategies they must develop to optimize the situation. Some may be doing much better than they thought and will thus need to protect their franchise, while others will find that they have little or no presence.

The opportunities are there in virtually any field one wishes to name. The skill comes in recognizing the opportunities and in positioning the products to achieve optimum impact.

7
A new advertising language—the creative approach

Monty Alexander

Introduction

Having demonstrated the power of the older population in marketing terms, and the opportunities that present themselves, our eyes turn automatically, and hopefully, to the creative advertising agency executives. How can these worthies who are accustomed to appealing to the jet-setting young, people with whom they identify very closely, redirect their energies and talents towards what up to now has been a rather uninteresting group? Monty Alexander tackles this challenge with a penetrating, amusing and meaningful examination of how the older person thinks, believes and is motivated.

Where it's at now—well, any minute now—is in the 50-plus bracket, that sturdy generation born just before the war, who survived evacuation, rationing, the 11-plus, a youth without telly, National Service. And what are they now? They are the new Mature Individualists.

They are at the height of their powers and looking to years, decades, of fulfilment ahead. And not, kindly note, to 'Retirement' but to 'Re-direction'.

Peter Fiddick, 'A New Golden Age'. *The Guardian* 14 March, 1988.

The emergence of the new elderly market poses the advertising industry with a communicational problem which might seem ironic to the onlooker.

The advertising industry has spent the last 20 years carefully re-positioning itself—and, in some instances, its clients too—deep into the world of youth and youth culture; the advertising business lifestyle has become the epitome of 'where it's at' in terms of economic, social and fashionable pace-setting.

How does such a trendy industry now get to grips with a lot of previously ignored 'new old' people, suddenly discovered to have lots of money to spend and lots of clear opinions of their own; not always the ones advertising agency people—particularly the creatives—necessarily want to hear?

However, what the advertising business has to find out now—and fast—is just what makes these 'Glams' and 'Woopies' tick? Otherwise, how can a typically young ad-creative of today, steeped in the streetwise culture of the late 1980s, launch himself into any meaningful, intimate, *persuasive* communication with an audience of men and women, any two of whom are old enough to be his parents, or even his grandparents?

To him, this is an alien world. This is cactus-land, where his regular cosmology of images often seems less than appropriate. What kind of role-models shall he use? What kind of lifestyle to proffer? What kind of slang? What kind of humour? How on earth to strike the right note in this communicational minefield, full of people all instantly able to detect—and reject on sight—the slightest whiff of youth-to-age patronage.

One obvious solution might seem as ironic as the problem. Why not recall some of the older creative people put out to grass at the time of advertising's last cultural revolution, when it turned to youth-worship? Those old guys and girls must surely be able to communicate effectively with people who are now their age-peers. They know the right words and catchphrases (they probably used them the first time around), they understand the over-50s mind-set and world-view—and could probably call on all kinds of idiomatic shorthand, unknown to the young, that would resonate in the minds of their target audiences.

Why not? The only weakness of these ex-creatives, summoned from their farmsteads, would lie in their inevitable lack of familiarity with some of the newer techniques and stylistic devices used by today's designers, particularly in the field of television graphics. But when we consider that most elderly viewers remain unmoved by a lot of the computerized special effects that they see on television, preferring those commercials and programmes that adopt a more 'real-life, narrative approach, with a clear beginning, middle and end', such a weakness hardly seems of major import.

1. The cohort effect

The first step towards an understanding of what motivates the elderly is to stop calling them Glams or Woopies. They hate the expressions; along with Empty Nesters, Wrinklies and all the other segmentational epithets, obviously dreamed up by (to the recipients) a load of marketing Yuppies, who can't help thinking in labels, given that they were weaned into a world full of such lifestyle tags as Hippies, Mods, Rockers and Punks.

The next step, if we're going to communicate meaningfully with older people, is to try to form some understanding of, and sympathy for, their current world-view. We can do this by monitoring the lives of one or more of the appropriate *age cohorts*.

An age cohort comprises any group of people born at roughly the same time—say, over a decade—in the same place or country. As a consequence, they have experienced the same major social, political and economic waves and upheavals at about the same age. Their lives were punctuated by the same crises. They share the same nation-memories: of music, films, entertainers, public figures, fashions and fads. And they encountered every new decade, each with its own particular 'flavour', at similar stages of their lives.

Over the past eight months, the Social Futures Unit and M3A (Marketing to the Third Age) have been engaging in a joint research study into 'The Cohort Effect': the ways in which shared lifetime experiences of members of an age cohort affect their *present-day* 'world-view'.

Although the principle of the cohort effect seems to hold true for every age group, we concentrate specifically on the decade-and-a-half between the ages of 50 and 65 years—the 'leading edge', so to speak, of the New Old. These are men and women all born in Britain between the years 1924 and 1939.

We hold discussion groups with members of this age cohort in different parts of the country. We probe into their past lives to assemble their 'Life-markers': the events, times, people, feelings, lifestyles (and life quality) that have figured strongly at some stage during the course of their lives.

We encourage them to talk about Life-markers within their remembered contexts: the dangers and privations of the War, the excitement of evacuation, images of the Blitz, of being poor, the discomfort of austere winters, rationing, Tommy Handley and the cast of ITMA, memories of Churchill's speeches, Henry Hall's *Guest Night*, Suez, the Beatles, the Profumo affair, the assassination of Kennedy, the later, more affluent years, and so on.

Also from the past we examine 'Link-lines': those sayings, catchphrases and quotes that seem to resonate in their minds beyond mere words, transforming themselves into veritable snapshots of an era:

> *Don't let the bastards grind you down.*
>
> *I'm alright Jack.*
>
> *Can I do you now sir?*
>
> *Don't you know there's a war on?*
>
> *You've never had it so good.*
>
> *Live now pay later. . . .*

We all store many such Link-lines in our memories. Group discussions seem to trigger their recall, in much the same way that group 'brainstorm' sessions stimulate the generation of new ideas.

We explore the Olympus of their all-time heroes and heroines, and the Hades of their villains, people who they have particularly admired within their lifetimes and perhaps tried to emulate in some way.

Turning to the present, we discuss dimensions in which they share a surprisingly homogeneous world-view: their opinions on the 'goods' and 'bads' of life today compared with 'yesterday'; the values they claim to esteem most highly—and the evils they most abhor; their everyday superstitions, maxims, 'myths' and 'live-by guides'.

We also investigate their own here-and-now view of themselves: why so many see themselves as *survivors*, as a 'bridge' generation, as lucky, and as sharing, to a greater or lesser degree, in the quality we intuit as the heritage of their particular age cohort: 'mature individualism'.

1.1 The nature of mature individualism

These 50–65-year-olds unanimously reject the word 'old' when applied to themselves, along with the derivatives and euphemisms that get clustered around it: 'old age pensioners', 'senior citizens', 'the elderly' and the like.

Nowadays, 50–60 just *isn't* old to them. They agree that it's perhaps late-ish middle-age (which, they acknowledge, began around 40) but they don't see proper 'oldness' occurring much before the age of 70.

'Maturity' is their own word—in a sense, their own euphemism. To them, it uncorks an attractively sentimental image-stream, compounded from ripe russet apples, vintage claret, patinated woodwork and polite, easy-going folk with the kind of lived-in faces that Norman Rockwell painted on his front covers for the *Saturday Evening Post*.

Mature individualism is the name that we—the investigators—have coined for the *Zeitgeist* that seems to be shared today by most members of this 50–65-year-old cohort.

'Individualism' isn't their own choice of word. It isn't even a quality they immediately claim for themselves; it's one that we as observers and researchers perceive in them.

The individualism of our definition springs from the hard-to-shock sophistication of their having—in their words—not only 'seen it all'; but actually lived through 'it all' as well.

This claim is undoubtedly true. In one lifetime, they've travelled further than any previous generation could have imagined. Quite apart from the hi-tech world in which they now find themselves—the world of Concorde, space travel, satellites and computers—they have *personally* travelled from the drudgery of wartime margarine and corned beef rations to the exotic food shelves of Marks & Spencer; from the chill nightly gloom of a blacked-out air raid shelter to the everyday luxury of central heating, bright lights and wall-to-wall television; from a drizzly week's holiday in Southend to two or three in sunbaked Corfu; from the overworked, hand-me-down family bike to the all-weather comfort of the family saloon, and—in monetary terms—the most dramatic switch of all: from their first £2–3000 newly-wed home to a world in which an ordinary family house can change hands at anything up to one-quarter of a million pounds!

One result of a lifetime straddling such enormous social and cultural extremes shows in their seeming composure when discussing, for example, the possibility of losing all this recent affluence in some sudden economic collapse. They appear more philosophic about this than younger age groups:

We've been through worse; at least we've got our health.

It is only money after all. There are more important things in life.

It was all a question of being in the right place at the right time.

We never really earned *the money in the first place.* (Reference to house prices.)

This last point touches one of the key concepts in the over-50s value system—the ethic expressed via such axioms as:

A fair day's work for a fair day's pay.

Effort brings its own reward.

You get nothing for nothing.

Hard work never killed anyone.

They have little respect for those they call the 'get-rich-quick brigade' —people who seem to be able to make a lot of money without apparently putting in an appropriate or 'fair' amount of effort.

For most of the age group, awareness of—and distaste for—this fly fraternity started with wartime memories of unpatriotic black marketeers. This candidate list was widened and the distrust nourished by stories of the exorbitant lifestyles seen to be conspicuously enjoyed during the 1960s by pop stars, property developers and the *demi-monde* of 'swinging London', many of whom appeared—in the eyes of the cohort—not to be working for their living in the *real* sense of the words, yet at the same time 'making more money than was good for them'.

Today too, in the critical eyes of the over-50s, 'these people' are still manifestly alive and well—and more pervasive than ever—in the persons of Yuppies and City slickers 'doing deals over the phone from their Porsches'.

1.2 Harnessing the cohort effect

Besides offering a number of socio-cultural insights, the age cohort study is primarily designed to explore further into this hitherto uncharted territory, to discover some basis for communication with this neglected sector.

Expressed in cohort terms, the creative/communication problem facing the advertising and marketing industries is this:

> *How does an industry, largely geared to the world-view of its own key age cohort (25–40), 'connect' successfully with the essentially different world-view of the 50-plus age cohort?*

The answer ought to offer more than the distribution of yet more nostalgia, which seems to be published more for the benefit of the style-hungry young than as any kind of reminder service for those who were present the first time around.

There is already a visual surfeit of images of the 1930s, 1940s, 1950s and 1960s—and the Second World War has surely been retrospectively re-fought enough times—as a glance into any colour supplement, comic, television or fashion magazine will confirm.

What is needed now is a method for tapping the present-day world-view of the cohort, *without recourse to Spitfires, Studebakers, Stewart Granger or skiffle*. One clear opportunity would appear to lie along the path of 're-cycled mythology'.

As part of their world-view, the 50–65 age cohort shares a number of 'myths' about 'the way things are'; about 'right' and 'wrong' behaviour on the part of society and themselves as individuals within it. *(Please note: my use of quotation marks is in no way intended as ridicule; simply to differentiate between stated belief and established fact.)*

Here is a short selection of some of these widely held 'myths'. Whether they turn out to be objectively true or false—or even true or false for other sectors of society—is irrelevant here. For this particular cohort, they knit together into a coherent and distinctive 'culture' of values and beliefs:

The Dunkirk spirit

That there is a strong unifying *esprit de corps*, just below the surface of the British which emerges only in moments of catastrophe. During these periods of heightened awareness, we—uncharacteristically—open up to, and help, one another, abandoning class and age differences and all the other (artificial) distinctions that keep us normally aloof and separate.

Recent examples include the Zeebrugge ferry disaster, the King's Cross fire, the Hungerford killings, the Lockerbie air crash and the Enniskillen Remembrance Day bomb—this last doubly meaningful because of its date.

They don't make them like they used to
That most consumer goods—especially motor cars, clothes, furniture and everyday mechanical objects such as clocks, watches and children's toys—were better made in the past, when people took a greater pride in their work than they do today.

Supporting this 'golden age' myth is the 'entropy myth': that the quality of everything steadily deteriorates (particularly aggravated at the present day as escalating 'city greed' for profits is seen to be forcing manufacturers to cut more and more corners in quality).

The Protestant ethic
That only hard work, over time, brings worthwhile reward and true satisfaction; there are no short cuts. This connects with previously-referred-to mistrust of the 'get-rich-quick brigade'. However, the cohort believes that this work ethic is well on its way out; that more and more young people are learning to 'grab what they can' in a 'go-for-it' world.

It is interesting to note here the well-known US advertising punchline of the brokerage firm of Smith Barney: 'We make money the old-fashioned way—*we earn it!*'

Life's too soft nowadays
That our children and grandchildren don't know the meaning of hardship, cold, discomfort, shortages, money, work, perseverance, etc., etc. This belief arises from the fact that most members of the cohort began life, by today's standards, in comparative poverty.

The myth is reinforced by memories of the Blitz ('Britain Can Take It') and the consequent rallying cry still used under pressure: 'If Hitler couldn't make us (do whatever it is), then (whoever) certainly can't!'

Manifestation of this myth-in-action can be seen during bus strikes, blizzards, hurricanes, etc., when it is usually the over-50s who still turn up for work.

Women and children first
That it is part of a man's role to protect/be chivalrous towards women and children. This is now an almost exclusively male myth—and diminishing even within this area. To most women—even those of the same age cohort—this belief is seen as the now obsolete cover-up for male chauvinism and idleness around the home.

You can't fool us
That—because of all we've seen and lived through—we can immediately spot the difference between a genuine 'first' and a load of 'bull'. This is

coupled with a parallel belief that the proportion of bull to real innovation is increasing exponentially year by year.

Hilary and Tensing, Roger Bannister, the Hovercraft, Concorde, the compact disc, video, Velcro, auto-focus cameras, duvets, the word-processor, low-alcohol lager; these are cited as examples of genuine firsts.

On the 'bull' list, they name Top of the Pops, many new savings and investment schemes, most fashion styles and stunts; and 'all that rubbish' on television to promote many supermarket and DIY products and stores.

1.3 The myth updated

The above are just a few of the rich store of myths that lies, entombed and ready-made, in the minds of the 50–65-year-old age cohort. Perhaps its most potentially valuable communicational attribute is that, given the right stimulus, *each myth carries its own built-in reflex/response*.

In other words, if I (advertiser) can convince you I'm talking about a 'Dunkirk-type' occasion, I can rely on *you* (cohort-member) to provide an appropriate emotional and behavioural response. Or, for example, if I can succeed in persuading you that it takes a certain amount of work, effort and perseverance to achieve something you desire, *you* will be triggered (at least emotionally) to rise to the occasion.

Perhaps the most exciting and creatively challenging part of the task is to discover ways of updating these myth-situations into present-day terms. This could both make them relevant, appropriate and credible for the cohort target audience—and, at the same time, interesting and meaningful to some degree to other overlapping audiences in today's multimarket world.

Several advertisers already set out to demonstrate that 'they *do* make them like they used to'—a conveniently timeless position for the crafted, luxury product. Such advertisers include both Parker and Cross pens, Rolex watches and most malt whiskies.

1.4 Traps to avoid

Alongside this substantial store of myths, rich with significance and ripe for updating, lie a number of 'counter-myths', equally emotionally charged, waiting to trap the unwary communicator confronted with mature individualism.

The *myths* of this cohort have been generated, in the main, through the experiences and observations of their own lifetimes. The *counter*-myths, on the other hand, are often compounded from contemporary hearsay and media gossip.

Better safe than sorry

The chief concern of all over-50s is for the security of their families, themselves and their properties in an increasingly dangerous world. Affluence, they ruefully agree, brings its own special worries with it, not the least being the responsibility for safeguarding an ever-growing life—full of material possessions.

The worries are compounded by their own feelings of vulnerability—of a physical strength turning to weakness with the passage of the years. The 'fear-myth'—eagerly nurtured by popular media—packs the streets of our inner cities with a Mayhew-like pantheon of contemporary low-life, proffering every conceivable manifestation of urban menace: muggers, vandals, street gangs, burglars, con-men, car thieves, drug addicts, pickpockets, loan sharks, 'lager louts', graffitists, football hooligans and dangerous drivers.

Within this context, it becomes easier to appreciate not only the elderly's high interest in security products of all kinds, but also their pathological dislike of any television commercial—and there are plenty, usually targeted to the young—that reawaken these fears; either by the casting of any persons reminding them of their rogues gallery, or by pitching its message in brash, over-familiar 'street language'.

Hi-technophobia

Another television style that seems to leave this cohort unmoved is that of computer graphics and/or electronic music. Virtually everyone presently aged over 50 years in the United Kingdom spent their early formative years in a pre-computer, pre-calculator world of book-learning, and pounds shillings and pence and mental arithmetic.

With their mental and emotional processes consequently schooled in such an imperfect, 'messy' environment, the over-50s usually react *against* the faultless geometry and glossy pattern-making of most computer-originated artwork and the 'inhuman' resonances of electronic music.

The music of their childhood came, too, out of a wireless set, and—if they were lucky—a 78 rpm gramophone. The older they are positioned today along the cohort spectrum, the more they try to avoid loud noise: 'heavy' pop music, top-of-the-voice dialogue, the unstoppable DJ.

Alongside hi-fi and commercial television came modern editing technology, compressing narrative into a tightly fused visual and aural 'flow'; where multilevel layers of meaning are obtained through unusual cutting, combined with the kind of impressionistic soundtracks that this age group often finds difficult to take in.

It comes as no surprise, therefore, to hear them lament the loss of the 'straightforward' type of storytelling film and commercial, 'with a nice clear plot—and dialogue you could hear as well as follow'. They thus appear to be an ideal audience for 'soap', whether in the guise of programmes or commercials.

1.5 Living with technology

We examine the over-55s' views on high technology itself, in the forms they mostly encounter it: the everyday household, office and leisure products that now play a large role in everyone's life. And here, the women of the age cohort appear to be more adept than the men, taking modern cookers, microwaves, programmed washing machines and dishwashers in their stride.

The men still hanker for pre-computerized machinery—perhaps because 'they don't make them like that nowadays'.

Both men and women proclaim their ineptitude in pre-programming the video recorder and usually rely on the job being done by a younger member of the household. There is irritation with video and hi-fi products of seemingly unnecessary complexity, which they see as a consequence of product designers and stylists being as young and high-tech as the audience they design for.

To them, such total disregard for any other than the 'fashion market', represents sheer negligence on the part of manufacturers. The over-50s see today's technological state of the art as being perfectly capable of simplifying the complexity of 'Concorde dashboard-type' control systems and making hi-tech products more user-friendly: 'remember the Pye Black Box'.

They cite auto-focus cameras and compact discs as examples of such breakthrough technology—products they see as appealing to both young and old in their presentation of 'sophisticated simplicity'.

1.6 'We're customers too'

As Sam Goldwyn might have said: '*Don't* include me out.' The idea of *not* inadvertently estranging this vast and affluent sector of the market makes an appropriately cautionary note on which to close a chapter on communication.

Much of today's advertising is given a 'young image' on no stronger pretext than the hoary, long-discredited advertising cliché 'catch 'em young and you've got 'em for life' or, even worse, because the agency, film crew, and often the client's marketing people are themselves young—and assume everyone thinks as they do.

A young image is a perfectly valid persona for certain products; but it is not a *sine qua non* of *all* products advertised on television and radio. And a young image acquired *at the cost of losing a lot of older customers* may well not be worth the price.

Yet such danger could be avoided by more attention to *semiotics*.

Semiotics—the science of signs and symbols—analyses the cultural 'lenses' through which we perceive the world around us, and extracts meaning from it. Semiotics studies how meaning is *made*. How one simple object can take on a range of totally different 'meanings', depending upon the cultural frame within which it is presented.

Take, for instance, a rose. After all, a rose is a rose is a rose. . . . But is it? Consider this same rose—and the different things it might 'mean' to, say, a flower arranger, a Labour politician, a Lancastrian, a lover, a Yorkshireman, a botanist, or a hay-fever sufferer.

In each of these instances, it is not the rose itself that changes. Objectively, it remains no more nor less than a particular botanical system. What changes, within each context, is the rose's 'cultural' meaning.

Given this understanding, it becomes easier to see how certain aspects of today's world, comfortably familiar to 20–30-year-olds, can take on entirely different—even nightmarish—associations and meanings, when seen through the cultural 'lens' of the 50–65—and older—age groups.

Call to mind some typical, current television and radio commercials. Think how often they feature such clearly alienating devices, for older viewers, as:

loud ('aggressive'?) rock music;
over-familiar ('pushy') presenters and voice-overs;
situations/people evoking ('threatening'?) aspects of street culture;
complex ('de-humanized') computer graphics and electronic music;
impressionistic ('hard-to-follow') sound and picture editing;

which raises a 64-dollar question: wouldn't it be worth trying to create a new, wide-audience *genre* of television commercial which achieves its effectiveness without overindulgence in such divisive devices—many of which, through over-use, have in any event slumped to the level of advertising clichés?

Maybe it's too difficult for today's agency industry. The danger, of course, is of producing bland 'committee commercials', so emasculated that they please nobody. But *if* it could be done creatively, sensitively and, above all, *effectively*, this would mean that although you are not appealing exclusively to the over-50s, you are at least not turning them off.

And for marketers of many mass-market products, it must make sound communicational sense to move some way towards acknowledging the cultural 'stance' of such a huge market sector.

The rewards could be tremendous.

References and recommended reading

Alexander, Monty, 'Check your cohort effect', *Executive Retirement*, November/December, 1988

Ibid., 'The coming of the post-employment market', *Executive Retirement*, September/October, 1988

Ibid., 'Illegitimis non carborundum!' *Executive Retirement*, January/February, 1989

Brooks, Richard, 'Woopie! It's the pippies', *Observer*, 17 July, 1988

Cohen, Anthony P., *The Symbolic Construction of Community*, Ellis Horwood & Tavistock Publications, London, 1985

Davies, Chris and Tom Kyle, 'The old-fashioned view of old age', *Marketing Week*, 19 February, 1988

Fiddick, Peter, 'A new golden age', *Guardian*, 14 March, 1988

Jackson, Alexandra, 'Growing older, getting richer', *The Times*, 10 September, 1988

Marketing to the Third Age, correspondence between M3A and 250 members of a mature panel (50–65-year-olds), recruited for market research purposes, 1989

McEwan, Feona, 'Granny generation seen as go-getters', *Financial Times*, 14 March, 1988

Middleton, Guy, 'The fabulous fifties', *Daily Mail*, 4 March, 1988

Ogilvy & Mather, TV advertising campaign for Smith Barney Harris Upton & Co., New York, 1979

Parkes, Christopher, 'Over 50s refuse to be pushed into spending', *Financial Times*, 4 July, 1988

Partridge, Eric, *A Dictionary of Catch Phrases*, Routledge & Kegan Paul, London, 1985

Social Future Unit/Marketing to the Third Age, qualitative studies into the cultural perceptions of 50–65-year-olds, 1988/1989

Symon, Penny, 'Youth gives way to Britain's old guard', *Daily Telegraph*, 6 August, 1988

Valentine, Virginia, 'Signs and symbols', *MRS Survey*, winter issue, 1988

Williamson, Cameron, 'A rosy outlook for over-50s', *Marketing*, 15 September, 1988

8
Older people in the United States—the invisible consumer market
Rena Bartos

Introduction

The realization that the older population constitutes a significant and growing market has occurred to marketers in the United States in advance of their counterparts in the United Kingdom and Europe. A considerable amount of the credit for this is due to Rena Bartos who recognized the wasted opportunities in this area some time ago and brought this to the attention of her colleagues in marketing, advertising and research. Rena describes the watershed events that occur in people's lives after the age of 49 years which define and shape their attitudes and behaviour more strongly than chronological age alone. These, together with such factors as leisure time, wealth and health define their potential as consumers. By uncovering these important concepts, Rena Bartos is helping to bring to light what has been, up to now, in the shadow—the invisible consumer market of the old.

It is no news that more people in the United States are living longer than ever before and that they are relatively more vigorous at chronological ages that used to be considered old. This trend towards longer life, combined with the social trends towards delayed marriage and fewer babies, has accelerated the shift towards an older population mix.

In recent years, the implications of the changing age composition of our population have been the subject of extensive public discussion. In 1979 the mandatory retirement age was raised from 65 to 70 years, and in 1986 Congress voted to ban mandatory retirement at any age. The congressional hearings that preceded that legislation were sparked by testimony about the intellectual and creative prowess of individuals in their 70s and beyond.

In spite of the fact that 18-year-olds were given the vote in 1971, it is the older people who turn out at the polls. They have organized politically through such vehicles as the Grey Panthers and the National Association of Retired Persons. They have developed political clout.

One of the concerns of older people is to overcome the myths about age and ageing that are so common to our youth-orientated society. The Executive Director of the National Council on Ageing warns that employers must re-think their stereotypes about older workers if able-bodied people over 65 years are to be able to participate in, and contribute to, the economic health of the United States.

In 1981 the White House sponsored a conference on the subject of ageing. One of the issues on the agenda was to develop 'policies to overcome false stereotypes about ageing and the process of ageing'.

At a recent conference in New York on the issue of age stereotypes, the spokesperson said: 'Old people are ugly, decrepit, stupid, forgetful, tooth-less, sexless after 65, ready to fall off the conveyor belt of life. . . . This is the way the media has portrayed us, the old, and we don't like it.' The speaker went on to say: 'We feel that the media is largely responsible for the perpetuation of this stereotypical image of the old. We are trying to change this because we believe that it is the cause of negative attitudes, prejudices, and behavior patterns toward the elderly.' She believes that the image of old people now being portrayed in television programmes and advertising is frequently unrealistic: 'First, there is the omission—we are the invisible people of videoland. Old people are not being shown in the media in relation to our actual number. . . . Second, older characterizations, when they do appear, are many times presented in distorted and stereotypical ways.'

So now, my colleagues in the advertising business and our clients, the advertisers, have one more 'ism' to add to our list of no–no's. We are already concerned about avoiding racism and sexism. Now, we must be concerned with ageism as well.

I personally believe that the way to overcome stereotyping in advertising and in the media is not through exhortation or social pressure, although these are the tools of social activists, but, rather, through awareness of social change and the impact of that change on the nature of the consumers with whom we communicate.

I think anyone concerned with advertising and marketing knows that none of us sits around in our meetings plotting how we can insult or demean various segments of our population. After all, no advertiser and no agency wants to insult its customers. So, if some of the portrayals of people in our advertising turn out to be perceived as stereotypical, it is through omission or lack of awareness rather than design.

The advertising that ends up on the screen and in the press is usually the result of a long, careful, marketing process. Therefore, I believe that the solution to stereotyping lies in the ways in which we define these basic targets for our marketing procedures. And most of us in advertising have, until very recently, concentrated the age definition of our target markets below the age of 49 years.

As a matter of fact, most marketing plans, and their resulting advertising campaigns, are based on definitions of the target group far below the 65-year age barrier which has concerned employers, social security specialists, and economists.

Until recently, it was difficult to find any advertising aimed at consumers over the age of 49 years (with the exception of those products designed to ameliorate some of the physical ailments of age). I personally propose to start my definition of this amorphous group at 49 years because it is at that point that previously unmet market opportunities begin.

Most definitions of marketing targets are usually expressed in demographic terms. However, the attitudinal assumption about what motivates the demographic groups may be observed in the advertising that is often the visible end-product of the marketing process. The advertising is beamed at the following audiences

Any housewife, 18–49
The key customer for all household products and foods is the housewife, who is the prime purchaser for the family. Her motivations are to win the husband's/children's approval of her competent, good housewifery; to do a better/faster job than her neighbour; to fool her husband/mother-in-law into thinking she's done something the hard way when in fact she has taken a shortcut.

Any male head of household, 24–49
The key customer for all big-ticket items—cars, business travel, financial services—is a man (husband and father). His motivations are status, that is, keeping up with/ahead of the Joneses; achievement; and protection of his dependants.

Any girl, 18–25
The key customer for cosmetics, perfume and fashion is the young, single girl. Her motivation, naturally, is to find a husband and settle down in her own ranch house. There the pattern starts all over again.

Any man, 18–34
The key customer for sports cars, beer, liquor, and toiletries is the young bachelor before he settles down. His motivation is to have fun; to find girls; and to avoid settling down for as long as he can.

The one characteristic that all the above marketing targets have in common is that *no-one is ever over 49 years of age*. This is truly an invisible market.

One of the problems in discussing an issue such as age stereotyping is that most people participating in the discussion are very imprecise in their definitions of age. Some start at 65 years, some at 60 years. I think that everyone in the marketing community knows that we have normally cut our target groups at 49 years. Therefore, I think it is useful to start with a very clear definition of what we mean by the 'older population'.

A paradox in this complex situation is that while we want to overcome ageism, we may be guilty of perpetuating it if we concentrate our redefinitions of the market on age alone. It is clear that people over the age of 49, or 60, or 65 years, or whatever age one wishes to start the definition of 'older', are simply not all alike. They are not a monolithic group. And, yet, in speech after speech and paper after paper I hear people referring to the 'older population', or the 'elderly', as though they were one homogeneous mass.

1. The invisible consumer market

When we shift perspective from the nebulous concept of 'older Americans' to the specifics of the invisible consumer market of people over 49 years of age, we learn that one out of four of our total population belongs to this overlooked segment. United States census forecasters project that by the year 2010 one out of three Americans will fall into this invisible consumer market. And by the year 2045 two out of five people in our country will be over the age of 49 years!

However, since most products are marketed either to adults or to children, it makes better marketing sense to examine the over-49s market in the context of the adult population, rather than to include children and teenagers in our comparisons. The present size of this segment warrants attention if only because of its sheer numbers. At the present time exactly 37 per cent of adults in the United States are over 49 years of age.

The year 2020 will be a watershed. In that year all the baby boomers will have passed the over-49 age barrier. At that point over-49s will constitute exactly 49 per cent of adults in the United States. At that time the over-49s market will be *the* market!

Why have marketers overlooked these consumers? Is it because they are not as good customers as the three in five adults who are over 19 and under 50 years? Why does age '49' represent the upper limit of consumer appeal to marketers?

In part, the answer might lie in many of the assumptions we have all held about the formation of brand choice in the early years of marriage, and the obvious volume potential represented by larger families. However, the facts of delayed marriage, divorce, and the realities of childlessness as an option have led to the proliferation of smaller households and childless households.

Only one out of every 10 households lives in the traditional mode of husband/head of household, supporting a wife who is a full-time housewife with at least one child under 18 years of age. And, if that traditional family has more than one child, it represents only 6 per cent of all households in the United States! Therefore, unless a marketer wants to sell to a declining segment, he must consider those consumers who live outside the traditional lifestyle.

In part, however, the over-49s market may be invisible because the people in it are so much a part of the mainstream. Except for the really elderly, they look so much like everyone else that we are not aware of them as an entity. Social commentators may talk about the 'greying of America', but our friends at Clairol have seen to it that there aren't too many Americans who are visibly grey!

2. Age is a continuum

This surface resemblance to the rest of the population may also be mirrored in the self-perceptions of people over 49 years of age. The evidence suggests that age is a continuum. People do not perceive themselves as different, unique, or set apart as they reach a particular age. Perceptions of the problems and satisfactions of life don't change abruptly at some specific birthday. There is a gradual decline in enthusiasm after 70 years and again after 80 years of age.

The continuum notion is reinforced by more evidence from the Harris study of ageing in America. Perceptions of the 'best years of a person's life' move up with age, with a certain nostalgic look back at the period just behind; and the older the group, the less likely they are to single out any particular age as 'the best'.

The paradox of the invisible consumer market is that although marketers have ignored people in this age group, age alone is not a sufficient differentiating factor to define the marketing opportunities within this diverse set of consumers. The greatest mistake any marketer can make is to generalize about 'senior citizens' or 'older Americans' as a group.

Even when we consider age, we must recognize that there are at least three generations represented among the over-49s. Some sociologists have defined them as 'the young/old', 'the old', and 'the old/old', with the conventional boundaries of 65 and 75 years as demarcation lines.

Clues to overcoming stereotypes may often be found in the semantics we use to describe a certain group. We can also obtain clues to the self-perceptions of 'older' people by observing their reactions to age-related labels.

The Harris study reveals that people over 65 years display a certain amount of discomfort and denial in responding to some of the more commonly accepted descriptive phrases. The 'labels' that they found most acceptable were: 'a senior citizen', 'a mature American', 'a retired person'. However, none of these was an overwhelming favourite. The descriptions that were overtly age-related were most rejected by this cross-section of people over 65 years of age. They clearly do not like to be identified as 'an old man/old woman', 'an aged person', 'an old timer', or 'a golden ager'.

However, not all people in this age group had the same reactions. There were some class differences in their responses. The lower- and middle-income groups endorsed 'senior citizen' as a strong first choice. This terminology was less appealing to the affluent. On the other hand, middle- and upper-income people were more responsive to being described as 'mature Americans' or 'retired persons' than were the less affluent at this age level.

These differences in response to the semantics of age suggest that all people over 65 years of age cannot be lumped together in one homogeneous group. The diversity of this segment is confirmed when we consider dimensions other than age in trying to understand the dynamics of this market.

The socio-economic conditions that shape people's lives are more differentiating than age alone in telling us whether people are satisfied with their lives. This is true at all stages of life: among young and middle-aged adults, among the 'young/old', and after 65 years of age. Apparently, it is better to be college educated and affluent at any age than to be young, uneducated, and poor.

To understand this segment as a market and to re-direct people's perceptions about ageing, we need to understand how older Americans regard age. At what age does old age begin? When do people think of themselves as 'old'? The answers to these questions seem to change with the age of the respondent. A flip answer might be 'someone who is 10 years older than I am'. Much of the verbatim testimony about age perceptions reveals that many older people do not really think of themselves as old. They say such things as: 'inside I still feel 21'.

When Harris asked people to name the age at which the average man or woman becomes old, there was not too much difference in the responses of people over and under 55 years. But only half could define old age in terms of some particular chronological age. And people over 55 years were less likely to define 'old age' in terms of a specific birthday. These people were more likely to use changes in their activities or in their life situations to denote old age: 'when your health fails,' 'when you stop working', or 'when women can't have babies'. Most said: 'it depends'.

2.1 The watershed events

There seem to be several keys to unlocking this market. If we move away from a generational definition to a situational one, we reflect the reality of change as recognized by people in this age group. The watershed events that occur in people's lives after 49 years of age may shape and define their attitudes and behaviour more sharply than chronological age alone. People's lives change and their needs as consumers change as they move through these inevitable life passages:

Empty nest
As children grow up and leave home, there is an automatic change in the way that family lives, and how they feel about their lives.

Retirement
Whether retirement is early or late, voluntary or involuntary, it represents a sharp and sudden change in living patterns, and a reordering of priorities.

Loss of a spouse
The death of a spouse marks another inevitable change from family life to life alone. The actuarial realities are that wives tend to outlive their husbands. This fact—combined with the empty nest phenomenon—means that a sizeable number of women in this age group have to learn how to live alone.

Ill health
There is no doubt that decline in health and vigour are inevitable accompaniments of ageing. Improvements in health care and preventive medicine are reflected in the increased chronological age of our population and in the greater number of people in relatively good health for more years than ever before.

The ways in which people handle the above changes in their lives are clues to their self-perceptions, their attitudes toward life, their motivations and potential as consumers.

2.2 The time/money/health equation

One reason why the over-49s market cannot be treated as a monolithic unit is that the potential adjustment of people to the situational changes in their lives is dependent on a multifaceted balance of time, money and health:

Time

The amount of time that people have available to them and the ways they spend that time defines them as consumers. People's perceptions of time change dramatically as their life situations change. Those people in this age group who are still actively engaged in work or family responsibilities have the pressures of too much to do, not enough time in which to do it, and very little time left over. On the other hand, at retirement, or the cessation of family responsibilities, time stretches out endlessly. The challenge or the opportunity lies in making productive use of this sudden gift of time.

Money

The amount of money available cannot give people the psychological resilience to meet change, but it does define the number and kinds of options available to them.

Analysis of the Harris Median Life Satisfaction Scores provides dramatic evidence of the difference that their degree of affluence can make in enabling people of any age to cope with life. As a matter of fact, unless the variable of income is considered, it is meaningless to generalize about older consumers as a group. The sizeable number of older people below the poverty level tends to depress any marketing analysis of people over 49 years of age.

Health

Of course, the state of their health determines the ability of people in this age segment to participate in the mainstream of life. No matter how comfortable their retirement incomes, the ability of older people to enjoy the leisure of retirement is dependent on their physical capacity to do so.

Table 8.1   The 50+ market in the United States

	% of 50+ age group	
Active affluents	35	
Active retired	19	
Homemakers	22	
High relevance to marketers		76
Disadvantaged	17	
Ill	1	
Other	7	
Low relevance to marketers		25

Source: Analysis of the US Bureau of the Census Current Population Survey, 1979–85

Considering both the watershed events of their lives and the objective facts of time, money and health, we have identified six segments among the invisible market of people over 49 years of age (Table 8.1). Three of these groups are not particularly relevant to marketers. They are 'the disadvantaged', 'in poor health', and 'others':

The disadvantaged
Since we are concerned with their market potential, it is realistic to isolate people below the poverty level from other segments of this age group. We refer to them as 'the disadvantaged' because they truly are. Their needs and problems are of more concern to students of society and designers of social programmes than to marketers.

In poor health
Fortunately, only a small minority of people over 49 years are incapacitated by poor health. Less than 1 per cent are defined by the census as ill or disabled. Their special needs and problems are relevant to the medical profession or to health care specialists, but not to marketers of general products.

Others
Finally, we come to the mysterious group labelled by the bureau of the census as 'others'. These are people who do not fit any of the occupational or situational designations we have devised. We honestly do not know anything about them. However, together with the sick they do account for 8 per cent of this age group.
    The three segments that do have real potential as customers for advertised products and brands are: the Active Affluents, the Active Retired, and the housewives.

The Active Affluents
The largest segment of over-49s are still at work and in the mainstream of life; 35 per cent of over-49s are in the group we term 'the Active Affluents'.
    From the perspective of the time/money/health equation, these people have limited time, maximum disposable income, and relatively good health. Since they are working, and at the peak of their earnings and professional achievements, they are also at the peak of their responsibilities. This means that time is at a premium. However, their family time is more flexible since, for the most part, their children are grown and gone from home. For these reasons, they have more discretionary money available than they did during the years of family formation. And the way they spend those discretionary dollars is a clue to their potential as consumers.

This is a group in transition. Its priorities are shifting. These changes may represent new marketing opportunities for the marketer attuned to their needs. The active careerists cannot escape the nagging realization that retirement is not too far off. This means that their financial priorities have changed from the responsibilities of building a home and educating children to anticipating the future. They are good prospects for investment programs, financial planning and annuities.

The shift from family life to the empty nest may create some emotional trauma, but it also means new living patterns for these suddenly childless couples. They now have the money and the opportunity to indulge in luxury travel, restaurants, and theatres. They want comfort and luxury when they travel, not backpacking, and, as they move out into the world of travel and entertainment, they have more need for fashionable clothing and jewellery.

The Active Affluents are in relatively good health, but they are concerned with the incipient ills of ageing. They watch their waistlines and their diets, for reasons of health and reasons of vanity. They are good prospects for spas, health clubs, cosmetics and beauty parlours. After all, one reason why this market is invisible is because only their hairdressers know for sure!

Although their chronological age sets them past the marketing cut-off age of 49 years, these Active Affluents don't feel or act old. They have adopted many of the 'new values' of living for today and not deferring gratifications for some non-specific future. They seek the full, rich life for themselves now and focus on self-realization and self-actualization. They are less likely than preceding generations to assume that their age dictates restrictions on the way they live.

In spite of the fact that we tend to think of the working women phenomenon as new and, therefore, more likely to involve young women, two out of five Active Affluents are women. Active Affluent men are somewhat more likely than Active Affluent women to be married (85 per cent to 63 per cent). This apparent anomaly may be due to the fact that men tend to marry women younger than themselves.

Four out of five of the married couples in this age group are also empty nesters, with no children under 18 years of age at home.

The big surprise is that three out of five of the married couples in this segment are two-paycheck couples, with both husband and wife in the workforce.

Not surprisingly, the greatest number of non-working wives are full-time housewives. However, 28 per cent of Active Affluent wives are married to men who are retired or are out of the labour force for other reasons. The great majority of Active Affluents live in a family orientated household arrangement. However, approximately one in eight lives alone. More than twice as many women as men live in these single-person households.

The Active Retired

Another key consumer group among the over-49s is 'the Active Retireds'. These are people above the poverty level who retired while they were still in good health; 19 per cent of people over 49 years of age are in this segment.

Depending on health, money, and attitude, retirement can be the beginning of a period of personal enrichment or it can mark the decline in participation in the mainstream of life.

By definition, these people should have more time for pursuing their hobbies and interests than when they were working. But, do they? In our work-orientated society the act of retirement is particularly traumatic. Many people define their identities in terms of the work they do. To quote one retiree: 'The puritan ethic says that if you don't work, you're not worth anything.' (Incidentally, this sense of identity has been one of the key motivations in the sudden flood of married women into the workforce.)

Retirement gives many formerly 'important' careerists a sense of rejection and loss. This is why volunteerism isn't as satisfying to many people as a paid job. They say such things as: 'If someone's work is valuable, he should be paid for it.'

The paradox of retirement is that it can be conceived as a well-earned rest or as rejection. This is reflected in two apparently conflicting trends. There has been a move toward early retirement in the past two decades. In 1979 the mandatory retirement age was raised from 65 to 70 years. The irony is that the more people are involved or committed to career or work, the more they desire to continue. On the other hand, there is evidence that people with routine, boring, or non-involved jobs welcome early retirement.

According to Harris, people over 65 years who are still in the workforce derive a greater degree of satisfaction from life than people of their age group who have retired. This difference is equally true when early retireds, between 55 and 65 years of age, are compared to their counterparts who are still employed.

Of course, enjoyment of life after retirement might be a function of whether retirement was chosen or involuntary. Almost half of the retirees in the Harris study said they 'did not look forward to stopping work'. Retirement has become a political, social, economic, and management issue. However, we are concerned with its impact on individuals as consumers.

Active Retireds don't want to be isolated from the mainstream of life. In spite of all the merchandizing of retirement communities, according to Roper most retired people prefer to live in a community among people of all ages. Only 5 per cent say they would like to live among people of their own age.

Not all retired people flee to condominiums in the 'sunbelt'. According to the study on retirement issued by the Conference Board, only 4 per cent of retireds moved out of their own communities after they stopped working. Another 20 per cent moved to another house in the same neighbourhood, or to a nearby community. The Harris study on ageing confirms this desire of retired people to remain a part of the larger community. Three out of four people aged 65 years and older said they would prefer to spend their time with people of all ages rather than be limited to associating with people of their own age.

This apparent resistance to being relegated to an age ghetto is reflected in part by the extent to which those eligible to do so participate in senior citizens clubs. Although half of the people over 55 years of age interviewed by Harris were aware that there was a senior citizens club available in their community, only 13 per cent actually visited one.

What is the key to successful retirement? Applying the perspective of the time/money/health equation, given enough money to live comfortably and in reasonably good health, time seems to be the crucial issue. After retirement, there is a new trade-off of time and money. When people are working, there is never enough time, so they pay for convenience, services and speed. On retirement, time is open-ended. There is a need to develop a structure to replace that imposed by working.

The way that the Active Retireds use their new-found time is the key to this segment of the over-49s market. Are they, in fact, the new pioneers of leisure? They have the time to take more leisurely trips than their working counterparts. They can travel by boat or take cruises rather than compress their holidays into one- or two-week long-distance plane trips. They have the time for exploring the offbeat experience of travelling by freighter rather than by conventional luxury liner or plane.

Three out of four Active Retireds are men. The dominance of men among this group as compared to the Active Affluents may be accounted for by their age. As the Active Affluents retire from the workforce, the higher proportion of women among them will also change the gender ratio among retirees.

Seven out of ten Active Retireds are married. The overwhelming majority of retired men (four out of five) are married, while three out of five retired women are not. Almost all the unmarried retired women are widows. Not surprisingly, the majority of the wives of retired men are full-time housewives. However, about one in six of retired men have working wives.

Five out of six Active Retireds live with members of their own families. However, one in six lives alone. Three times as many women as men in this group have set up house on their own.

The housewives

One out of five people over 49 years of age are women above the poverty level who are full-time homemakers. However, to understand their potential as consumers, we have to consider their personal situations as evidenced by the following three facts:

1. Three out of ten of these over-49s housewives are married to Active Affluents.
2. One out of three are the wives of men who are Active Retireds.
3. Another one out of three are not married. Most of these are widows.

For married housewives, the watershed events that occur 'over 49' are when the children leave home, forcing them to adjust to the empty nest, and the change that occurs in their husbands' lives when they move from work to retirement.

For the *wives of the Active Affluents* the moment when children leave home can lead to the shock of no longer being needed. On the other hand, given good health and enough money, the empty nest frees them to join their husbands in indulging in the fun of luxury restaurants or travel. It also gives them time for a little personal indulgence and pampering.

When does a housewife retire? Housewives are truly an invisible market because there is so much continuity in how they spend their time. We speculate that the key to this market is both the time/money/health equation and their living situation.

There is probably less difference in the lives of full-time housewives after their husbands retire than in the lives of retired men and women because their time is structured by the routines of housekeeping. Margaret Mead has said: 'One reason that women live longer than men is that they continue to do something they are used to doing, whereas men are abruptly cut off whether they are admirals or shopkeepers.'

Since women tend to live longer than men and may marry men somewhat older than themselves, the watershed event of the loss of a spouse creates more *widows* than widowers. For these women the trauma of emotional loss is intertwined with an abrupt situational change not unlike that of involuntary retirement. To the extent that their life patterns have run along traditional lines, their husbands and children have been the focal point of their lives. Their role in life (and concomitant source of gratification and identity) has been that of wife and mother.

In a sense, as they become widowed, these women also become suddenly unemployed. As with retired people, their time is open-ended. Also, their ability to cope with this change in their lives probably started long before their husbands' deaths. If they had hobbies and interests and active social lives when their husbands were alive, they were probably able to continue and expand some of those activities when thrust upon their own resources.

Another element in their adjustment might have been the extent to which they participated in family decision-making while their husbands were alive.

For example, most of these women grew up in an era when it was not considered feminine to be knowledgeable about money. Unfortunately, the more protective the husband and the more he sought to shelter his wife from the crass realities of the marketplace, the more likely she would be to find the transition to financial responsibility a traumatic one.

We speculate that the time/money/health equation is crucial to the kinds of lives that members of this group lead. There is a world of difference between the blue-haired dowagers travelling on the QE2 and isolated old women living on meagre incomes.

3. Demographics

3.1 Age

Active Affluent men and women are the youngest segment of over-49s. Two-thirds of the group are under 60 years and one in five are aged between 60 and 65 years. On the other hand, the majority of Active Retireds are over 70 years old. Only a handful took early retirement in their 50s. A small proportion are under 65 years. Retired women tend to be somewhat older than retired men.

There is a real continuum in the ages of the three segments of housewives, as follows:

1. Those whose husbands are still in the workforce are the youngest. Three out of five are under 60 years. Their median age is 58 years.
2. The wives of retireds are older. Their median age is 68 years.
3. The widows are the oldest group of all, with a median age of 74 years.

3.2 Education

Active Affluents are the best-educated segment of over-49s, as the following four points show:

1. Active Affluent men are slightly more likely than Active Affluent women to have graduated from college or gone on to post-graduate studies.
2. Retired women are somewhat more likely than retired men to have had some college or post-graduate education.
3. The wives of Active Affluents are slightly better educated than the wives of retireds.
4. The widows are more likely to have limited education.

3.3 Income

As might be expected, Active Affluents are by far the most affluent group among the over-49s population. Active Affluent men enjoy a higher level of household income than Active Affluent women.

However, the real difference between them becomes apparent when one examines personal income. The personal income of Active Affluent men is twice that of the women in that category. Retired men are slightly more prosperous than retired women.

There is a real continuum in levels of household income among the three categories of housewives, as follows:

1. Not surprisingly, the wives whose husbands are employed also enjoy a high level of household income.
2. The wives of retired men obviously share the income levels of their husbands.
3. The widows are the least affluent of all the segments among the over-49s market.

We have seen that the various segments within the over-49s population have different motivations and different demographic profiles. The way they actually behave in the marketplace and in their selection of media is evidence of their diversity.

Two marketing questions will help define this group, as follows:

1. How do members of this group spend their time?
2. How do they spend their money?

The answers to these questions should help us to look beyond the stereotypes.

3.4 How do they spend their time?

Daytime television

In case you've wondered who is watching the tube during the day, it is retired men and women and housewives over 49 years of age. Retired women and widows are the biggest fans of daytime television, followed by married housewives and retired men. Active Affluent men and women are clearly not responsive to television during the day.

Prime-time television

All segments of consumers over 49 years of age are above the norm in watching prime-time television. Both Active Affluent men and women are strong supporters of this medium. However, retired women and retired men are the greatest fans of television in the evening.

All the over-49s groups of housewives are above the norm in watching television. However, widows and wives of retired men are more likely than wives of Active Affluents to watch prime-time television.

Radio

Radio seems to be of less interest to consumers over 49 years of age. Active Affluent women are at the norm in listening to radio. However, all other segments of the over-49s market tend to be light listeners.

Magazines

Over-49s consumers are all below the norm in reading magazines. However, Active Affluent women and wives of Active Affluent men are more likely than any other over-49s segment to be supporters of magazines.

Newspapers

Newspapers are an important medium for some segments of the over-49s market. Active Affluent men are most likely to be very heavy newspaper readers, followed by Active Affluent women, retired men and wives of Active Affluents. Retired women and wives of retired men are just under the norm in reading newspapers, while widows are least likely to be active newspaper readers.

Outdoor

All the over-49s segments are somewhat below the norm in time spent outdoors. However, Active Affluent women are relatively more likely to see billboards. They are followed in this by Active Affluent men and retired men. Retired women and all three types of housewives are least likely to pass billboards in the course of their activities.

3.5 How do they spend their money?

We might also ask how the over-49s handle their money and how they spend it.

Investments

The over-49s are relatively affluent and financially sophisticated, and their investment behaviour shows it. While only 18 per cent of all adults invest in stocks, bonds, or in securities other than savings bonds, more than 25 per cent of over-49s are likely to make such investments.

Active Affluents of both sexes are the heaviest investors. The change to retirement brings a lower level of investment activity, although Active Retireds are substantially above the total population norm in this area. Retired men are almost twice as likely as retired women to be active investors.

Credit cards

The total group of over-49s is also more likely than all adults to own credit cards, either the travel and entertainment (T&E) variety, or bank cards, thanks almost entirely to the Active Affluents. Active Affluent men are especially heavy subscribers to T&E cards, and they own bank cards as well. Active Affluent women are more likely to own bank cards than T&Es. And housewives who are married to Active Affluent men are more likely than the population as a whole to say 'charge it' with either type of card.

Luxuries and cars
Active Affluent men constitute a unique market within the total over-49s group. They not only invest in stocks and bonds, they are the only segment above the norm for buying diamond rings, and they are slightly above par in collecting coins. They are also active drivers. They drive more miles than the average and are more likely to own two or three cars, compared with the overall population. Not surprisingly, they are good customers for tyres and car wax.

Active Affluent women, however, are unlikely to buy diamonds, but they do buy costume jewellery. They are more likely to own only one car. They are also particularly good customers for luggage.

3.6 Beyond the rocking chair
The over-49s market represents a wealth of opportunities for those marketers who are willing to challenge their own assumptions about age. Marketing procedures that have succeeded with the usual target groups can be applied just as effectively to these relatively undiscovered consumers. This chapter is not intended as an exhaustive inventory of all the products and services of possible interest to those aged over 49 years. Nor is it intended as a blanket recommendation that every advertiser of every product category automatically concentrate on consumers over 49 years.

Judgements as to products' potential should be made on a case-by-case basis. Those marketers who conclude that outdated assumptions about age may have deprived them of valuable customers can take action. The potential market for various products and services among the over-49s segments can be determined. Practically minded marketers must challenge the underlying assumptions on which past target definitions have been based. The process for doing that is as follows:

1. Re-examine the assumed target
Information about particular groups or segments of consumers is available from the US Census Bureau or Bureau of Labor Statistics. Professional journals, daily newspapers, and the rest of the popular press are constantly full of reports on changing attitudes, values, and lifestyles. Many companies have access to public opinion polls that track social beliefs and attitudes. Does a review of the data suggest that some groups within our society are changing or are in need of being segmented?

2. Evaluate the marketing potential of new target groups
An objective appraisal of the market behaviour of newly identified consumer groups can indicate whether they buy or use products differently from their neighbours, and whether their media behaviour is distinctive. An appraisal of their product use can tell us the potential that each group represents for a particular category or brand.

3. Develop a fresh perspective
When new insights suggest the need for new demographic questions, they should be included in all ongoing and future studies. In the case of the over-49s market, occupational status, sex, income, marital status, and occupation of spouse are required to identify the relevant market segments described.

4. Explore the attitudes and needs of the new groups
Hypotheses about potential targets can be identified by reviewing masses of data and can then be verified by re-analysing existing data to determine whether the targets' marketing and media behaviour is unique. To understand why these redefined targets behave as they do, we need to make use of qualitative exploration.

5. Redefine marketing targets
If the facts suggest untapped opportunities, the kinds of marketing procedures that have worked well in the past can be used to go after the new target groups.

We have the know-how. We have the data. The relationship of time, health, and money, and watershed events can help us to segment this monolithic mass into meaningful markets. The challenge for marketers is to break away from their absolute fixation with the 18–49 age group.

If we abandon the comfortable rocking chair way in which we have always defined our targets, we might discover significant opportunities within the invisible consumer market.

References and recommended reading

Aspen Institute for Humanistic Studies, 'Attitudes and technologies: striving to match new electronic information products and services to the needs and interests of elderly people', Communications and Society *Forum Report*, 1988
Ibid., 'Case by case: examining applications of new electronic technologies to meet the needs of elderly people', Communications and Society *Forum Report*, 1988
Ibid., 'Seniornet: toward a national community of computer-using seniors', Communications and Society *Forum Report*, 1988

Bartos, Rena, 'Beyond the rocking chair', *Marketing Review* pp. 15–23, June, 1988

Bluestone, Mimi, 'What's new in products for the aged', *New York Times*, 2 December, 1984

Brown, Patricia Leigh, 'For the aging and disabled, products they can use', *New York Times*, 21 April, 1988

Carnegie Corporation of New York, 'Human resource implications of an aging work force', The Aging Society Project, New York, November, 1984

Collins, Glenn, 'As more men retire early, more women work longer', *New York Times*, 3 April, 1986

Conlin, Kelly, 'Wooing older consumers: a diverse, vast market', *New York Times*, 27 November, 1986

Davis, Brian, and Warren French, 'Exploring advertising usage segments among the aged', *Journal of Advertising Research*, 29, pp. 22–29, February/March, 1989

Day, Ellen, Brian Davis, Rhonda Dove, and Warren French, 'Reaching the senior citizen market(s)', *Journal of Advertising Research*, 27, pp. 23–30, December/January, 1987

Dychtwald, Ken, and Joe Flower, *Age Wave: the challenges and opportunities of an aging America*, Jeremy P. Tarcher, Los Angeles, 1989

Edmondson, Brad, 'Inside the empty nest', *American Demographics*, pp. 24–29, November, 1987

Gollub, James, and Harold Javitz, 'Six ways to age', *American Demographics*, pp. 28 *et seq.*, June, 1988

Greco, Alan J., 'The elderly as communicators: perceptions of advertising practitioners,' *Journal of Advertising Research*, pp. 39–46, June/July, 1988

Louis Harris and Associates, *Myth and Reality of Aging in America*, 1976

Health Insurance Association of America, 'The prime life generation: a report describing the characteristics and attitudes of Americans 50 to 64 years of age, Washington DC, 1985

Keane, John G., 'Our aging populace: advertising implications', *Journal of Advertising Research*, 24, (December/January), RC, p. 10–RC, p. 12.

Konrad, Walecia, and Gail DeGeorge, 'US companies go for the gray', *Business Week*, pp. 64–67, 3 April, 1989

Lazer, William, and Eric H. Shaw, 'How older Americans spend their money', *American Demographics*, pp. 36–41, September, 1987

Lewin, Tamar, 'Business and the law: forced after-70 retirements', *New York Times*, 28 January, 1986

Linden, Fabian, 'New money and the old', *Across the Board*, pp. 43–49, July/August, 1985

Lumpkin, James R., and Troy A. Festervand, 'Purchase information sources of the elderly', *Journal of Advertising Research*, 27, pp. 31–43, December/January, 1987

Lumpkin, James R., Marjorie J. Caballero, and Lawrence B. Chonko, *Direct Marketing, Direct Selling, and the Mature Consumer: a research study*, Quorum, New York, 1989

Mandese, Joe, 'The new old', *Marketing and Media Decisions*, pp. 32–40, April, 1989

New York Times, 'House bars a set retirement Age', 24 September, 1986

Ostroff, Jeff, 'An aging market: how businesses can prosper', *American Demographics*, pp. 26 *et seq.*, May, 1988

Petra, Peter, 'Marketers mine for gold in the old', *Fortune*, pp. 70–78, 31 March, 1986

Pifer, Alan, and Bronte, Linda (eds), *Our Aging Society: paradox and promise*, W. W. Norton, Dunmore, PA, 1987

The Roper Organization, 'Retirement: reward or rejection?', Conference Board, p. 23, New York, 1977

Ibid., *The Roper Reports*, vol. 77–7, p. 9, New York, 1977

Schewe, Charles D. (compiler), 'The *Elderly Market: selected readings*, American Marketing Association, Chicago, 1985

Schick, Frank, *Statistical Handbook on Aging Americans*, Oryx Press, Phoenix, Arizona, 1986

Simmons Market Research Bureau, Custom Analysis, 1979, 1983, 1985

US Bureau of the Census' *Current Population Survey*, March 1985, March 1979

US Bureau of the Census, *Population Estimates and Projections*, May 1984

US Department of Health and Human Services, *Aging America: trends and projections*, 3rd edn, Washington, DC: GPO, 1988

Wasik, John D., 'Going After the Gray Dollars', *New York Times*, 5 February, 1989

9
Marketing to the over-55s— the locational element
Peter Sleight

Introduction

Marketing is about communicating with target audiences, and this requires knowledge of where they are located. In recent years, the science of geo-demographics has done a great deal to make this technique more systematic and accurate by linking detailed census information with marketing data.

In this chapter Peter Sleight describes how the locational techniques of geodemographics can be used to ascertain the areas in which old people are most likely to live, and also to make the kind of differentiations between different types of old people which are essential if marketers are to reach their intended targets.

1. Introduction to the locational approach

As a generalization, marketing men (and women) are very ambivalent about the locational element in marketing. On a personal level, it is clearly important; wearing their 'shopper' hats, they will decide where to go to buy their groceries, their clothes, their household durables. They may not consciously rationalize *why* they go to those particular shopping centres, any more than do shoppers in general. However, back in the office with their marketers' hats back on their heads, they will probably revert to looking at their markets in national and (at best) regional terms, paying little regard to the local aspect.

The main exceptions to this general rule are the retail marketers, and the direct marketers. Retailers need to know the importance of store location, and in my experience they do; arguably site location is so vital to success in retailing that to ignore it is to risk disaster. Direct marketers, who may not have branches, of course, tend to recognize the value of location because they have been schooled in the practice of *targeting*. They know it is possible to reduce the wastage inherent in (for example) 'blanket' mailings, by targeting prospect mailings into localities and neighbourhoods where they will find the greatest probability of successful sales conversions.

The growth of direct mail is itself an indicator of the way things are changing. In recent years direct mail has emerged as a mainstream medium of communication; although it is relatively expensive in terms of cost per message delivered (compared to, for example, television) the fact that it can be targeted very precisely means it may well be more cost-effective where the target market is specific rather than general. The 55+ market (and its subsets) come into this category—it is a specific, rather than a general, audience. My point is not that direct mail is therefore the automatic media choice, but rather that a *locational* approach is appropriate when considering this market. It is evident that this section of the population is not evenly spread throughout the counties, towns and neighbourhoods of the United Kingdom; some of the concentrations (the 'retirement areas') are well-known, but considerable variations exist which are probably less obvious. We will examine the pattern of relative penetration later in this chapter.

The technique of locational analysis of demographics is generally known as 'geodemographics'—a fusion of geography and demographics; and the source of raw data in the United Kingdom is the census of population. This is a massive resource, which has been used extensively for planning purposes by central and local government, but has been relatively little used by the marketing community. This is partly cultural—it is not the way in which marketing has 'traditionally' been conducted in this country—and partly a matter of ease of access. It required the advances in computing technology which have been experienced in the last decade to unlock this potentially very valuable data source.

The Office of Population Censuses and Surveys (OPCS) who collect and publish the census, divide the whole of England, Scotland and Wales into 130 000 small areas called 'census enumeration districts' (or EDs), each containing on average 150 households. Each ED is designed in such a way that it may be covered by an enumerator on census day; therefore the rural EDs, which may cover large geographical areas, will tend to contain less than the average number of households, while the dense urban EDs will contain more than the average.

The OPCS distribute census forms to every household in every ED and collect the replies; they process and publish the statistics at an ED level, being extremely careful to protect personal privacy in doing so. They produce a very comprehensive analysis of age, sex, household composition, employment status, occupation (therefore social class), housing conditions, car ownership; as I said, a massive resource. The census data are produced as a series of 'counts' for each ED; there are 4000 counts for each ED in England, Scotland and Wales, plus a further 1500 special counts applying to Scotland and Wales. Thus the data can be visualized as a matrix with 130 000 EDs on one axis, and 5500 counts on the other; over 500 million cells of data for the 4000-count matrix alone!

Hence the need for computing power. It takes significant resources to manipulate data of the magnitude involved here. Fortunately, computing technology has made great strides in the last decade; real costs of computing power have decreased significantly, and the advent of personal computers and workstations has brought computing onto marketing practitioners' desks. A recent development in census analysis has been the introduction of PC-based analysis systems which enable marketing companies to conduct their own geodemographic analyses. Admittedly, they are unlikely to have the need or the capability to manipulate the whole of the raw census dataset; they will prefer to use 'packaged' data, probably for units of area the size of wards or postcode sectors (about 2000–2500 households on average).

Thus awareness of the merits of this locational approach is increasing, as is the capability to implement it, either via census bureaux or on an in-house system. How may the data be used?

2. The locational approach—using the data

Two issues need to be addressed when deciding how to use census data to locate the 55+ market. The first concerns the units of area to be used, the second relates to the way the target market is defined and the statistical methodology by which it is identified.

The choice of units of area ranges from television regions (or standard regions) at one end of the scale, to census 'neighbourhoods' at the other. Clearly, this choice influences the complexity (and therefore cost) of the task, and needs to be influenced by the way in which the resultant information will be used. For example, taking the two media mentioned in the introduction: Independent Television and direct mail: in the case of Independent Television (ITV), one might choose those ITV regions which contain the highest concentrations of population 55+; for direct mail purposes, that solution would be much too crude, and one might select those census neighbourhoods which have the highest concentrations of 55+. The averaging effect, or 'dilution' of the target market naturally tends to increase with greater size of unit area.

There are two distinct 'geographies' to choose from. (And unfortunately their boundaries do not match!) One is administrative geography, the other is postal geography. From 'top–down', administrative geography starts with counties and reduces through Local Authority Districts and wards; counties may be aggregated to the 12 standard regions, and wards may be broken down into EDs. The boundaries of these areas, with the exception of EDs, are fairly well known and used—for administrative purposes at least, although less for marketing purposes than was once the case.

Postal geography is becoming increasingly popular for sales and marketing purposes. No doubt one strong reason for this is that addresses can be readily allocated to any unit of postal geography once they are 'postcoded'. This is because of the hierarchical nature of postal geography (Table 9.1). For example, Pinpoint's office postcode is SE1 8UL, which locates it to:

SE   = postal area, London south-east
SE1   = postcode district
SE1 8   = postcode sector
SE1 8UL = full unit postcode

Table 9.1 also indicates that there are approximately one-and-a-half million unit postcodes in total, with an average of nearly 15 addresses per postcode. Of course, this average disguises a wide range of cases; there are many postcodes with a single address attached, and some unit postcodes contain hundreds of addresses.

Thus, given two distinct forms of geography, how may they be related, one to the other? The demographic characteristics will be derived from the administrative geography (wards or EDs) courtesy of the OPCS; but one may decide that (say) postcode sectors are the ideal units of areas for one's purposes—for defining sales territories, distribution areas, or retail catchment areas.

If both sets of boundaries have been 'digitized' (transformed into strings of map references in a computer-readable form), then it is possible to relate

Table 9.1   UK postcode system

	Postal areas	Postcode districts	Postcode sectors	Unit postcodes
Total in UK	120	2 700	8900	1 500 000
Average households	183 000	8 150	2500	14.7
Average population	466 000	20 750	6300	37.3
(Example postcode, SE1 8UL)	SE	1	8	UL

Source: Pinpoint Analysis

postal geography to administrative geography. In order for the 'translation' to be accurate, it should be performed on the lowest units of area. So if postal geography is to be used for the analysis, and if postcode sectors are the chosen units of area, then census EDs will need to be 'fitted' to postcode sector boundaries. This is achieved most accurately if ED boundaries are also held in 'digital' form; failing that, the 'centroids' of EDs—grid references of the population-weighted geographical centres, which are supplied by the OPCS—may be used. This may all sound rather technical; but in geodemographics and related geographical analysis, care taken with the input data makes a great deal of difference to the output information, as we have found repeatedly.

The second issue to be addressed when deciding how to use census data to locate the 55+ market is the choice of methodology by which it is identified. Briefly, we can either use the 'raw' data, or we can use some derived product, such as a neighbourhood classification system.

The former is the simpler. By expressing the desired target market (say, all adults 55+; or, all adults 65+; or even all households containing one or more adults of over 55+, etc.) as a *penetration*, it is possible to analyse all units of area accordingly, to identify where the concentrations of this particular market may be found. Let's take, as an example, a requirement to locate population aged 55+ at a census neighbourhood (i.e. ED) level, within a defined ITV region. First, the census agency concerned would identify all the EDs within that ITV region boundary, and would then compute the percentage of total population within each ED who were aged 55+. Then the EDs within that region would be sorted in rank order on that criterion. The marketer could specify the required output in one of two ways: either as a list of EDs taken from the top of the ranking until the required number of households had been reached (for mailing, or door-to-door distribution); or specified as EDs with a concentration of (say) 70 per cent or more of the population aged 55+. Either way, a distribution table could be produced to guide the marketer as to how many EDs (and households) came into each penetration band. The neighbourhoods in question could then be identified, either on computer maps, or by converting them into street lists or addresses.

The other way of identifying target markets by geodemographic means, and indeed the way most familiar to marketers, is via census-based neighbourhood classification systems such as ACORN or PiN. These classification systems are produced by the census agencies in question selecting a number of census variables (41 in the case of ACORN, 104 in the case of PiN) and using these variables in cluster analysis to identify census EDs which have the most in common with each other, as against those that are different in character. The sorts of variables used will normally include such things as age bands of population, family composition, housing amenities and number of rooms in the household, social class of head of household, car ownership, type of tenure, etc. From these variables, a multifaceted picture of the type of neighbourhood in question may be built up.

Given that the age dimension is the critical factor in our considerations, we will be particularly interested in the neighbourhood types that contain high proportions of the population aged 55+. It should be noted that the proportion of 55+ population which can be located by this method is always likely to be lower than that found by adopting the single-minded approach detailed in the preceding method; this is because in the preceding method, presence of a 55+ population is the only criterion of selection, whereas using a neighbourhood classification system, the other variables present in the cluster solution will have effectively 'diluted' the single variable in which you are interested (i.e. 55+ in this case). This point will be illustrated in the next section of this chapter, together with the other methods discussed here.

Another type of classification system has been developed since the launch of the 'general purpose' classification systems such as ACORN and PiN. This is a 'market-specific' classification for the financial services industry, branded FiNPiN (financial PiN). It uses another input to its methodology, that is, indicators of financial activity, taken from National Opinion Polls' (NOP's) Financial Research Survey (FRS). In a sense, the methodology has 'fused' information from FRS with census characteristics to enable neighbourhoods to be classified by their level of financial activity. Thus, using FiNPiN, we can identify those neighbourhood types containing a high proportion of 55+ age group, and we can relate this to their financial activity in general; and by cross-tabulating the FRS survey, we can study their propensity to purchase specific financial products and services. Again, more of this later.

Finally, in this section, one more census-based method for discovering more about one's market. This uses a product which we could call a 'derived variable'. If you apply a statistical method known as Principal Components Analysis (PCA) to a set of census variables, the PCA will identify a set of components which represent the underlying 'themes' in the data. For example, wealth versus poverty, rural versus urban, etc. Pinpoint used PCA as an interim stage in the development of PiN (the 104 'raw' census variables were subjected to PCA, and the resultant components were put into cluster analysis). The component emerging from that process, which accounted for the largest proportion of variance in the data, grouped together variables such as owner occupation, high social class, multiple car ownership per household, households containing seven or more rooms, etc.; the 'trappings of wealth'. We labelled this principal component the 'Wealth Indicator', and use it frequently as a neighbourhood discriminator. It is different from the neighbourhood classification systems such as ACORN, PiN, or even FiNPiN, because it 'scores' neighbourhoods on a single dimension, that is, on the presence or absence of the trappings of wealth. All the EDs in England, Scotland and Wales are scored on a scale of 0–100, 100 being the wealthiest end of the scale. Thus, if one had applied the first method of targeting mentioned in this chapter (ranking EDs on penetration of population aged, 55+), one could also apply the wealth indicator as an 'overlay' —so that one might specify (if one wanted to reach 'wealthy' 55+ people) that you were interested in neighbourhoods containing, say, 60 per cent or more penetration of people aged 55+, with a wealth indicator score greater than 70.

3. Geographical analysis in practice

So much for an overview of the methodology—now the practicalities of locating a 55+ target market. As an illustration of the dispersion of the 55+ market, the map in Fig. 9.1 shows the penetration of this age group by county. This map is generated by the computer, based on an analysis of census data and the 'digitized' county boundaries. The counties are grouped into six 'quantiles'; the higher the penetration of the 55+ age-group, the denser the shading.

The penetration of the 55+ population within counties is in a range between just over 20 per cent, and 37 per cent penetration (the national average is 26 per cent). The counties in the highest penetration range include Norfolk, East and West Sussex, the Isle of Wight, the west country counties of Dorset, Somerset, Devon and Cornwall; the counties in west Wales (Gywnedd, Dyfed and Powys) and the Scottish Borders. Of these, only three (Dorset, the Isle of Wight and East Sussex) have penetrations of over one-third of total population being 55+. It is always comforting for one's prejudices to be confirmed, of course; East Sussex has the highest concentration of over-55s, at 37 per cent of the total.

To illustrate the point made in Section 2—about the effect of unit of geographical area on concentration of target market—we will take the highest-penetration county of East Sussex, and break it down into smaller geographical areas in order to examine the effect of this on locating the biggest concentrations of the 55+ market. First, postcode sectors: these areas average some 2500 households each. We conducted a postcode sector ranking exercise on the county of East Sussex and studied the statistics resulting from this exercise.

The postcode sector with the highest concentration of 55+ population in East Sussex occurs in central Bexhill, with over 70 per cent of the population of this sector being aged 55 years or over. The penetration figures then drop

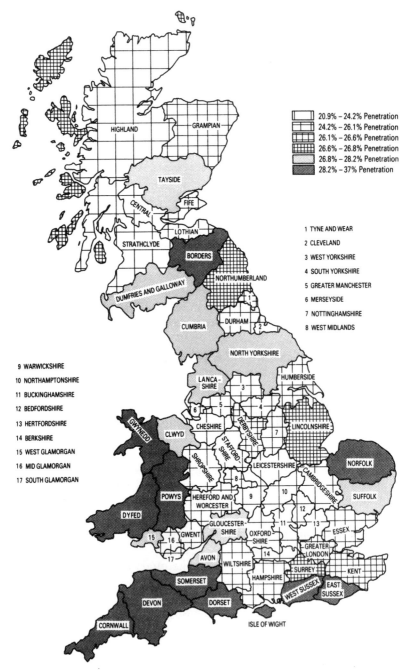

Fig. 9.1 Location of the over-55s by county in the UK (*Source*: Pinpoint analysis)

fairly rapidly; the 10th highest penetration sector has a penetration of just over 55 per cent. As a matter of interest, the lowest penetration postcode sector in East Sussex—south of East Grinstead—has a penetration of only 18 per cent, so quite a range exists even within this one county. Where are the highest penetration sectors? Once again, the areas are fairly predictable: central Bexhill, south-west Eastbourne, central Eastbourne, Pevensey Bay, Eastdean—all above 59 per cent penetration. The other five sectors in the top 10 are all in the same part of the world—a charming sounding sector comprising the villages of Alfriston, Litlington, Wilmington, Jevington and Folkington (near Eastbourne); two sectors in Hove; Collington, near Bexhill, and Gotham—surely not Gotham City?!—no, a village near Bexhill.

So by reducing the size of our geographical unit from counties (nationally —which gave a penetration range of 20–37 per cent) to postcode sectors (within East Sussex) we have improved our 'concentration' of over-55s to 70 per cent, in the top ranking sector. What about census EDs, the smallest areas for which these statistics exist? We ranked all the census EDs within East Sussex, produced grid reference locations for them, and studied the results. There are 1663 census EDs in East Sussex. Three of them have 100 per cent penetration of people who are 55+ (admittedly, two of those being very small EDs!). The top 10 EDs have penetrations higher than 90 per cent, the next 23 EDs being higher than 80 per cent; then the penetrations drop fairly rapidly, and level out into a more gently sloping distribution curve with a long 'tail'. This is fairly typical of this type of analysis. Once again, let us study where the very highest concentrations of 55+ populations are occurring. Four of the top 10 EDs are in Hove! Three are in Eastbourne, one each in Bexhill and Brighton. The only 'odd one out' in the top 10 most concentrated 55+ neighbourhoods—the only one *not* at the seaside— occurs at Uckfield, well inland. This 'pinpointing' of a target market means that in this particular situation, if one wanted to send a message (say, a mailshot) to an audience of predominantely 55+, one's wastage would only be of the order of 8 per cent on the first 1000 letters mailed.

Now the final section in this chapter deals with ways in which one may use this facility. Before that, however, I will illustrate my other point from Section 2, concerning different methodologies. We have considered the use of a single census variable (age 55+) as a means of locating concentrations of this age group, at different sizes of geographical area. The other possibility, of locating over-55s via a neighbourhood classification is rather less efficient. For example, at the 25-fold breakdown of the country, the PiN neighbour-hood type with the highest proportion of 55+ population is PiN-type 'j', labelled 'comfortable retirement areas', and accounting for 1.74 per cent of total population and 2.31 per cent of all households. On average, 53 per cent of the population in this PiN-type neighbourhood are aged 55+. The second highest penetration of 55+ population is in PiN-type 'i' ('council flats with pensioners') where the 55+ population accounts for nearly the same proportion of the total (actually 52.7 per cent). So these PiN types represent a *fairly* efficient way of targeting the over-55s (and one knows many other things about the characteristics of these areas, from the other variables which went into the solution) but one cannot be as single-minded in targeting high concentrations of over-55s as one can by ranking on that specific age variable, as we saw earlier.

A similar analysis using FiNPiN (the financial market segmentation system), at the 40-level breakdown of the country, shows that the highest penetration of '55 pluses' is in FiNPiN-type 30, who are described as 'financially conscious' (rather than active), 'basic product users' and are 'elderly in small council dwellings'. Nearly 60 per cent of the population in this FiNPiN neighbourhood type are aged 55+. It is straightforward to ascertain the financial products and services used by this and other FiNPiN types, by cross-tabulating the Financial Research Survey by FiNPiN. Methodology has been developed to convert this information into a means of measuring the potential for defined products and services within areas.

4. How the information can be used

We can now locate the target market, both at a 'neighbourhood' level, and expressed as a penetration within any type and unit of geography that we choose. The way in which we use this information obviously depends on the type of organization we represent, and our objectives.

If we operate a retail or quasi-retail network of supply points we may want to review the extent to which our existing branch network is covering the market in the optimum way. Do we have stores or branches accessible to all the viable concentrations of target market residential neighbourhoods? Are we represented in the 'catchment areas' within which they shop and/or travel to work? Are we over-represented in some areas, and where are the best areas within which to consider opening new branches? In the case of retail operations which have a broad target market (i.e. an appeal across the whole of the socio-demographic range) mere *numbers* of potential shoppers may be the issue; but the more segmented the appeal, the more crucial it is to locate one's target market, and match supply to latent demand as efficiently as possible. Naturally, there are other issues affecting retail location, such as presence or absence of competition, relative costs, etc.—these variables can be modelled and their influence quantified. But the fundamental issue is the quality and quantity of the defined target market available to the site in question, and thus the derived market potential.

Following on from the retail locational issue, the retailers or their suppliers may want to stimulate local demand by means of local marketing activity, such as leaflets, coupons, etc. Again, these may be targeted most cost-efficiently by using the techniques described in this chapter. It is possible to compute the comparative costs of, on the one hand, 'blanketing' an area with leaflets, as against distributing them selectively into targeted areas. The largest cost element will generally be the print and production cost of the leaflets themselves. The cost of distributing them will normally be a smaller element; there is a price premium to be paid for selective distribution, and for the market analysis which drives this, but in most markets, there is still a net saving from those leaflets which were *not* wasted in areas of low potential. The usual convention is to target leaflets and coupons using postcode sectors as units of area; postcode sectors are put into rank order on their penetration of the target market (as illustrated in Section 3) and either a cut-off penetration is decided, below which the wastage would be unacceptably high, or a quantity for distribution is decided and sectors are chosen from the top of the ranking list until that quantity is reached.

Now let us take the case of a supplier of goods to the over-55s market, which supplies those goods through retail outlets not controlled by the supplier in question. For example, goods sold through grocery chains, variety stores or chemists. Obviously, the supplier cannot influence the siting of the stores themselves, although he may be able to influence which stores within a given chain should stock his products. You may say that ideally from his point of view, *all* stores in a chain should stock; this is not necessarily so if the result is a disappointing level of sales overall, leading to a danger of the retailer 'delisting' his product. So it helps to know the disposition of his target market, and the identity of the stores which best serve this target market. Knowing this, the supplier is in a good position to have an informed dialogue with the retailer, suggest which stores should stock his products and what his estimate of market potential within that store catchment should be. In these days of the rapid growth of electronic point of sale data capture—i.e. 'scanning' tills (EPOS), the retailer is in an increasingly strong position in terms of relevant data; the supplier owes it to himself to equip *himself* with best available market data, to stimulate a discussion rather than to receive an instruction! The supplier can also use the data to recommend, say, leafleting activity in selected sectors within the catchment areas of stocking stores, to stimulate throughput and to enhance mutual business with that retailer.

Of course, suppliers of consumer goods through intermediate retailers may operate through sales forces, who would themselves find the market information very valuable in establishing a 'base' potential against which they could organize sales territories, set sales targets, and proposition retailers. However, this application of the data would only be one side of the coin; the other would be concerned with building and maintaining a consumer brand franchise—advertising and promotion. The locational element has its part to play in this very important area of activity.

The question of media choice is outside the scope of this chapter, although the subject has been touched on in the introduction, in the context of television 'versus' direct mail (in reality it should be 'horses for courses'!). However, in the quest for cost-efficiency which so characterizes most marketing departments these days, it is helpful to be able to quantify apparent potential wherever possible. So take a simple example of television; we saw in the county map example that the penetration of the 55+ market is very uneven across the country. This impinges on the ITV regions, and by being able to quantify this, one can calculate how much of the overall market one may reach if the budget does not allow national coverage, but requires selectivity. Which combination of television regions delivers the most cost-effective result? Naturally, the calculation would need to incorporate television audience research data to establish the age profile of television programme viewing, together with costs per thousand of over-55s viewers; but the whole calculation should be predicated on the penetration of the 55+ market within each television region.

The same principle can be applied to Independent Local Radio areas. Some of these areas contain much higher proportions of the over-55s market than others, not surprisingly. This is a relatively easy calculation to conduct. Of course, the real question should relate to the listening profile of each ILR station, and the numbers of over-55s listeners which each generates; if such research exists and is reliable, then clearly it should be used, but if not, then an approximation can be made by applying national listening research profiles to a local audience profile.

Media research will provide readership profile information for the national press, and magazines—this is covered comprehensively elsewhere. However, the opportunity for *regional* editions seems to be growing, and here the locational analysis approach has a contribution to make. Indeed, it is essential to a recent development—the facility to carry localized 'tip-ins'; this may prove to be a very significant development. The availability of good data to support the regional press is also increasing and, here again, 'geodemographics' is a part of the mix. Free local newspapers are a special case because, unlike the 'paid for' newspapers, the 'frees' can specify precisely their circulation areas, and therefore these areas can be analysed precisely. Many of the 'frees' offer a postcode sector-based targeting facility, so one may apply the technique of postcode sector ranking, against a defined target, as mentioned earlier in this chapter.

Clearly, by its very nature, poster location lends itself to a neighbourhood-based targeting approach. Research demonstrates that it is not simply a matter of siting posters within areas that contain concentrations of (say) a 55+ audience—due note has to be taken of pedestrian and vehicular traffic flows—but, nevertheless, the locational approach can and does generate information about travel-to-work and travel-to-shop flows, which can be applied to poster audiences just as they are to retail analyses. Again, it is a matter of knowing first of all where your target market *lives*!

As a general rule, the more localized the activity, the more helpful the locational approach will be. If that sounds obvious, then—as I mentioned in the introduction to this chapter—the fact that it is not universally used is probably more an issue of tradition and technology than of acceptance. Technology has made possible commonplace techniques that were little used 10 years ago.

One area of marketing where the above is demonstrably true is the direct marketing sector. Customer databases, personalized laser printing, precisely targeted communications, telephone response systems; this whole sector has developed apace. And direct mail can deliver the ultimately localized target—an individual address. No doubt the future will bring electronic targeting to individual addresses too (our views on that may depend on whether we are buyers or sellers—see for example cold-canvass telephone selling!). In parallel with these developments, the data protection lobby has been established and formalized and certainly the vast majority of practitioners recognize the need to act responsibly and sensibly.

Direct mail can make perhaps the maximum use of locational techniques. We saw in Section 3 an example where a mailshot could be targeted at an over-55s audience with very little wastage, by 'picking off' census neighbourhoods with very high concentrations of this audience. The same principle is employed when using neighbourhood classification systems. For example, a Building Society wants to sell a new term share product; as a subscriber to the FRS research survey, it can establish which FiNPiN neighbourhood types have a high propensity to purchase this type of product. So, the Society can segment its own customer file, and mail customers for other products who are in the appropriate FiNPiN-types of neighbourhood, with information about the new product. Or it can mail names selected from the electoral roll on the basis of their FiNPiN neighbourhood types; thus improving the chances of a relevant mailing.

The way in which geodemographics should be used, the caveats and cautions, is a large subject in its own right, and is outside the scope of this chapter. One issue not touched, for example, is the matter of how address data (i.e. postcode-based data) are linked to census data; this can be a very fraught area, where precision is vital. Pinpoint is making a contribution to this practice by compiling the Pinpoint Address Code, or PAC, database; when complete this will be a computer file of all the addresses in the country, with precise locations. Thus, while not attempting to go into this sort of detail, the aim has been to provide an overview of the way in which this locational approach to marketing is relevant and applicable. Conceptually, it allows a user to know the locations of all the relevant neighbourhoods in the country, and how they fit into shopping patterns, media boundaries, administrative and health regions.

References and recommended reading

Journal of the Market Research Society, special issue: 'Geodemographics', vol. no. 1, Market Research Society, London, January 1989

10
Television and the older population
Bernard Bennett

Introduction

The use of television increases with increasing age. The over-55s spend far more time watching television than on any other waking activity, and have a keen interest in what they see. Bernard Bennett, Head of Research at London Weekend Television, looks at the large quantity of information which is available on the relationships between older people, television and the advertising which appears on television. He argues that the importance of television to the old has been underestimated by most marketers, who adapt their television advertising mainly to the requirements of the young. As a result, the advertising is less effective with old people than it ought to be, which in view of their major marketing importance clearly shows that opportunities are being missed.

One-quarter of Londoners are 55 years of age or more, and can expect to survive for another 20–25 years of active life, in many cases with a fair degree of affluence. They epitomize the group that Professor Sandra Van De Merwe dubbed the GRAMPIES in her article in 'Business Horizons' in 1986. GRAMPIES is an evocative acronym that stands for growing *r*etired *a*ctive *m*onied *p*eople *in* an excellent *s*tate. In 1988, London Weekend Television interviewed a number of mature Londoners about their GRAMPIES' lifestyles, and we reproduce in the Appendix some of their edited statements which have many pointers for manufacturers' current and future communication strategies. To neglect the implications will mean missed business opportunities. The sample is not, and does not pretend to be representative. What we believe it gives are a few insights into the attitudes and behaviour patterns of older people in the modern world—attitudes and behaviour patterns that are very different to those of their parents and very different to the generally received opinions in the commercial world. The questions were posed by a professional LWT reporter with the backing of a camera team in the Waterloo area of London.

These GRAMPIES are articulate. Communicating with them is not difficult. They are receptive and well-disposed to television and television advertising. The single most important topic talked about in the lives of the 55–64-year-olds is television. At 50 per cent this is way above the next most frequently mentioned subject, the cost of living (37 per cent). This finding stems from ITV's continuous survey of advertising issues that has been conducted by National Opinion Polls (NOP) since 1980. The study is known as the Television Omnibus Monitor (TOM), and interviews over 3000 adults throughout the United Kingdom each year to very high standards of sampling methodology. Some results are given in Table 10.1.

In contrast, advertising is not a salient topic of conversation; it is mentioned by no more than 3 per cent of the sample, rising only slightly to 4 per cent among the 55–64 group. Advertising is not at the forefront of GRAMPIES' concerns, and does not of itself arouse their passions and

Table 10.1   Main talking points amongst different age groups

% saying things talked about most	All adults	Age group		
		16–54	55–64	Over-65
Television programmes	48	49	50	43
Cost of living	35	23	37	45
Health and welfare services	25	23	29	32
Gardening	16	11	23	28
Law and order	16	14	20	21
Newspaper articles	21	23	18	17
Unemployment	14	14	18	10
Clothing and fashions	20	24	18	7
You and your family's health	19	19	16	20
Sport	23	25	16	19
Bringing up children	24	31	16	8
The present government	18	18	15	22
Education	19	24	13	9
Neighbours and workmates	19	24	10	9
Politicians	8	8	8	10
Religion	5	5	6	7
Trade unions	4	4	4	3
Big business	3	4	4	—
Advertising	3	3	4	3

Note: Ranked on 55–64-year-olds
Source: Television Omnibus Monitor

Table 10.2   How do you feel about advertising in general?

% saying:	All adults	Age group		
		16–54	55–64	Over-65
Completely/mostly/slightly more favourable	54	57	47	46
Neither favourable nor unfavourable	27	26	31	28
Slightly more/mostly/completely unfavourable	17	16	20	22
Don't know	2	1	2	4

Source: Television Omnibus Monitor

interests. This is not to say that they regard advertising unfavourably. Quite the contrary (Table 10.2). Their positive feelings (47/46 per cent) outweigh their negative feelings (20/22 per cent) in the ratio of more than 2 to 1. This is less pronounced, admittedly, than for the under-55-year-olds, but it is still high.

Attributes of advertisements seen on television by the GRAMPIES (Table 10.3) are: that they are entertaining, 44 per cent; a good way of finding out about new products, 41 per cent; are truthful, 34 per cent; and are informative, 35 per cent. There are negatives of course, which advertisers need to be aware of and, hopefully, try to avoid in their own campaigns.

Table 10.3   Opinions of advertisements seen on television

% saying television advertisement very/fairly often (are):	All adults	Age group		
		16–54	55–64	Over-65
Positives				
Informative about the products	34	32	39	30
Truthful	34	33	32	36
Good way to find out about new products	42	42	41	41
Entertaining	44	44	44	43
Negatives				
Interfere with your enjoyment	38	38	44	34
Cause annoyance	25	22	31	28
Same ad on too often	59	57	61	61
Treat you as foolish	41	43	43	36
Misleading	31	31	34	31

Source: Television Omnibus Monitor

Excessive repetition is the strongest complaint, 61 per cent; followed by being treated as foolish, 40 per cent: and by being misleading, 33 per cent.

In comparison with the other main media, television fares well. Over two-fifths of the GRAMPIES like television advertisements 'a lot of a little', in contrast—in descending order—to 28 per cent for magazines, 22 per cent for newspapers, and 15 per cent for radio. This in part will be a reflection of the fact that television advertising is regarded as entertaining as well as informative. Other media do not have this advantage in anything like the same degree.

Besides the evidence of the ITVA national TOM Survey, LWT's unilaterally commissioned research from Marplan in the London ITV area among 750 housewives in 1987 provides strong confirmation of the high status of television advertising when matched against the press, radio and posters. Not only was it reinforced that television was generally the most useful for the GRAMPIES, 69 per cent; the best at finding out about new products, 76 per cent; and the most truthful, 55 per cent; but also that television scored better for specific product information including: healthcare, 54 per cent; buying and cooking food, 55 per cent; electrical goods, 49 per cent; and cosmetics and toiletries, 54 per cent. Only on home improvements was it marginally behind the press, 42 per cent compared to 44 per cent.

In the United Kingdom press readership tends to decline with age among the various main groups of publications (Table 10.4), particularly for the general weekly, and for the general monthly and women's monthly magazines—by about 1/10th for the GRAMPIES compared to the under-55-year-

Table 10.4 Newspaper and magazine readership

Reading any	Adults		
	Under-55s (%)	55s and over-55s (%)	Difference (%)
Daily, morning	69	66	3
Evening	31	29	2
Sunday	74	73	1
General weekly	42	31	11
Women's weekly	26	26	—
General monthly	41	30	9
Women's monthly	37	24	13

Source: National Readership Survey

Table 10.5   All day summary, at home and available to view, Network, April 1984

| All day | All | | 55–64 | | Over-65 | |
(06.00–01.00)	%	Index	%	Index	%	Index
Mon–Thu	42	95	52	118	56	127
Fri	40	91	50	114	53	120
Sat	45	102	53	120	54	123
Sun	54	122	60	136	58	132
All week	44	100	53	120	55	125

Note: *Index*—all week, all indexes = 100%
Source: AGB Attwood Survey

olds. Possibly this is not surprising as it is another area where younger people's interests tend to be emphasized at the expense of the older element. An ageing readership profile is something to be avoided, not welcomed, by most publishers. Specialist publications are obviously the exception, but these have been dealt with by Stephan Buck in Chapter 5.

In contrast, as Stephan Buck has also demonstrated, and so will only be recapped here, television viewing increases dramatically with age and reflects the good opinion of the medium held by the GRAMPIES. It also reflects that over virtually all days and times of the week, the over-55s age group are at home and available to view to a far greater extent than the total population. An AGB Attwood survey in April 1984, throughout the United Kingdom, using a diary technique commissioned by the ITVA, showed that their index of availability to view over all-time segments on all days was mostly between one-fifth and one-third higher, and that this advantage was most pronounced at weekends (Table 10.5). The achieved sample over 16 days, ending Monday 23 April 1984, included over 7000 respondents, and availability to view was defined via the following two factors:

(a) actually viewing television or a video cassette for at least half of the appropriate quarter-hour or half-hour periods;
or
(b) it would have been possible and convenient in the respondents' judgements for them to have watched had the programmes been attractive enough.

Except for Saturday, when the figure falls to the two-thirds mark, as many as three-quarters of GRAMPIES are at home and available to view in the

Table 10.6 At home and available to view, Network, April 1984

	6	7	8	9	10	11	12	13	14	15	16	17	18	19	·20	21	22	23	24	1	2
Mon–Thu		06.30 09.30			09.30 12.30				12.30 16.00			16.00 18.00		18.00 22.30				22.30 24.00		After 24.00	
All %		31			25				32			50		67				43		25	
55–64		41			38				46			56		75						36	
65+		43			46				54			62		76				56 50		31	
Fri																					
All		30			24				31			48		64				43		26	
55–64		40			34				43			53		72				55		37	
65+		42			41				53			59		73				49		31	
Sat		06.30 09.30			09.30 12.30				12.30 17.00				17.00 23.00					After 23.00			
All		32			39				43				60				33			
55–64		41			42				53				68				43			
65+		40			45				57				69				36			
Sun		06.30 09.30			09.30 12.00				12.00 18.30				18.30 19.30	19.30 22.00		22.00 24.00		After 24.00		
All		32			45				57				67	71		48		25		
55–64		43			52				64				75	79		60		36		
65+		40			52				65				74	77		54		30		

Note: Available to view = watching television for at least half a period, or not watching but it would have been possible and convenient to watch.

Source: AGB Attwood Survey

peak evening segment between 1800 and 2200 hours (Table 10.6). No less than two-fifths are available in the early morning (before 9.30 a.m.), and nearly a third are still around at midnight.

Higher availability translates into higher viewership. The over-55s age group view over half as much again as the under-55s age group in the average week. In London, in the week ending 13 March 1988, for example, the respective figures were 28.5 hours and 15.9 hours. These are high figures on an international yardstick. The United Kingdom would be near the top of a league table of country-by-country comparisons.

For many years LWT have been conducting what have become known as 'Commercial Recognition' studies. These comprise hall tests where samples of respondents are exposed to showreels of current advertisements, but with the brand names, insignia and other identifying features blanked out. Nevertheless, a high proportion of the sample can usually correctly recall and recognize the brands, and from these figures an index of correct commercial recognition can be compiled. For example, in 1987 450 house-wives were tested in five different locations in LWT non-overlap territory, yielding a correct overall recognition score, averaged across 18 advertise-ments of 38 per cent (Table 10.7).

Typically, the GRAMPIES have a lower commercial recognition index than the younger respondents. For this particular 1987 study, the index for the over-55s age group was 75. The shortfall is substantial, but not wildly dramatic. Sometimes the hypothesis is advanced that the reason for the lower over-55s group performance is that they are less alert and mentally slower than the young. The television advertising message, it is argued, has less impact on them. There are reasons to doubt this contention, as will become clear a little later, but whatever the explanation, the shortfall is compensated for by the fact that television's 'share of voice' is equally as strong among the GRAMPIES as it is among the young. Substantiation for this claim stems from a similar series of BMRB studies in the September/October periods in the London area among samples of 1100–1200 adults, asking for mentions of 'outstanding advertisements' seen or heard in the last four weeks. These studies have consistently given television advertisements by far the highest proportion of mentions, or 'share of voice', compared with mentions for advertisements in newspapers, magazines, posters and radio. Among the over-55s group, television's share of voice was no less than 89 per cent in 1988, and has been at a similarly high level in previous years (Table 10.8).

One possible reason for the GRAMPIES' lower recall of specific advertisements, compared to the under-55-year-olds, is not declining physical faculties, but the fact that advertisers neglect them in their creative treatments. This is a very serious point. In 1987, a Gallup survey (Table 10.9) found that 56 per cent of the over-60s age group agreed with the statement that 'manufacturers of products are really only interested in young people and don't care about the needs of the elderly'.

Table 10.7 Commercial recognition

	Index of commercial recognition
All	(38%=) 100*
16–24	134
25–34	126
35–44	105
45–54	100
Over-55	75

*38% = 100: over showreel of 18 advertisements
Source: LWT/Marplan Survey, May 1987

Table 10.8   Recall of 'outstanding advertisements' by media

% saying outstanding advertisement seen in last 4 weeks		Penetration				Share			
		All	16–34	35–54	Over-55	All	16–34	35–54	Over-55
Any	1986	59	64	60	50	100	100	100	100
	87	59	67	53	54	100	100	100	100
	88	59	65	60	52	100	100	100	100
Television	1986	51	65	53	45	87	87	88	90
	87	50	57	48	45	86	86	90	83
	88	51	56	52	46	87	86	86	89
Posters	1986	4	5	3	2	6	8	6	4
	87	3	4	2	2	5	7	4	4
	88	3	4	4	1	5	6	6	2
Newspapers	1986	2	1	4	3	4	1	6	6
	87	3	1	2	5	5	2	4	9
	88	2	2	1	2	3	3	2	3
Magazines	1986	1	1	2	0	2	2	3	1
	87	1	1	1	0	1	2	1	1
	88	1	2	1	1	2	3	2	2
Radio	1986	1	2	0	1	2	4	1	1
	87	1	2	1	1	2	3	1	1
	88	1	2	1	1	2	3	2	2

Source: BRMB Survey

Table 10.9   Over-60s perception of manufacturers' interest

% response to: 'Manufacturers of products are really only interested in young people and don't care about the needs of elderly'

	All over-60s (%)
Agree	56
Neither agree nor disagree	16
Disagree	28
No answer	1

Source: Gallup, 1987

Readers of this text will largely recognize the marketing importance of the over-55s, or will at least be beginning to give them greater consideration. Yet the advertising industry at large does not do so. The neglect is widespread, except in age-specific products, and is quite startling in the United Kingdom. What prompted an investigation of this neglect was an article in the American *Journal of Advertising* which conducted a content analysis of 814 advertisements shown over a 36 hour period on the three main US networks in November 1985. The main finding was that 'while 12 per cent of the current US population is over 65 years of age, only seven per cent of the advertisements containing people utilized elderly characters. In the majority of commercials the elderly are not typically cast in major roles.' (Table 10.10.)

A similar content analysis has now been carried out by the LWT Research Department, over the weekend of 4–6 August 1988 in London for all ITV and Channel 4 commercial transmissions. The findings confirm the US study (Table 10.11). Of 1421 advertisements transmitted only 77, 5.4 per cent, had elderly people (those who appeared to be over 55 years) playing a major role. This is way below their population weight of 27 per cent. It is not surprising that the GRAMPIES do not identify with the characters in the majority of commercials, and therefore have a somewhat lower recall level for individual commercials. A major role is defined as where an elderly person is the main character portrayed or where presence and speaking occurred throughout the advertisement. In the remaining 11.9 per cent of instances where they appeared at all, the elderly were portrayed as playing only minor roles in which they did not speak, or were seen as supporting characters only, or were in background roles where, again, they did not speak and were seen only briefly.

Table 10.10   Advertisements with non-elderly and elderly people by network

Network	Advertisements with non-elderly people	Advertisements with elderly people	Total advertisements with people
ABC	263 (92.9%)	20 (7.1%)	283
CBS	208 (92.9%)	16 (7.2%)	224
NBC	194 (93.3%)	14 (6.7%)	208
Totals	665 (93.0%)	50 (6.9%)	715

Source: US *Journal of Advertising*, 1987

Table 10.11   Content analysis: LWT/CH4

Total advertisements transmitted	1421	=	100%
Role played by elderly people (those appearing, 55 years or older)	Any		17.2
	Major role		5.4
	Minor role		9.4
	Background only		2.4
	None		82.8

Source: LWT Research Department Survey, London, 5–7 August, 1988

The way the elderly are cast in advertisements was also examined (Table 10.12). A key difference between the two studies was the depiction of the elderly as advisors, as people turned to for their knowledge and experience. Nearly two-thirds (65 per cent) of the American commercials containing old people cast them in an advisory capacity, as valued for their wisdom; in the United Kingdom this figure dropped to under 1/10th (9 per cent). Many reasons could be advanced to explain this difference, including the subjectivity of our classification procedures, and the fact that the studies were carried out nearly three years apart. Possibly the fashion has shifted to a more humorous approach in the interim, because UK advertisements show a preponderance of light-hearted treatments, 39 per cent compared to 13 per cent in the United States.

An examination of the product fields featuring the elderly in commercials (Table 10.13) showed that one-third were related to finance, one-seventh to food, and just under one-tenth each to cars and drink. At least the financial houses recognize the importance of the elderly in their markets. Advertisers

Table 10.12   Content analysis: type of character portrayed

	Advertisement with elderly people	
	UK, 1985 Over-55s	US, 1985 Over-65s
Total advertisements with elderly	17% = 100	17% = 100
Elderly depicted as		
Advisors	9	65
Information receivers	29	15
Comical/humorous	39	13
Feeble/confused	8	7
Other	16	—

Source: LWT Research Department

Table 10.13 Content analysis: product fields
featuring the elderly

Category	Advertisements with elderly, UK 1988 (17% = 100)
Finance	34
Food	15
Cars	10
Drink	9
Tobacco	5
Other	28

Source: LWT Research Department

and agencies in many other markets need to absorb the implications of these results. The cult of youth can be taken too far; age discrimination has its penalties. Those who make a conscious effort to appeal to the over-55-year-olds should benefit from higher awareness of their commercials and by tapping a greater portion of the 31 per cent share of disposable income that the Henley Centre estimated the GRAMPIES to account for in the United Kingdom. If the old can identify with the lifestyles portrayed in commercials to a higher degree than is now possible, then the advantages to the advertiser should follow automatically. At present, the old are not being wooed or being cultivated at a level commensurate with their importance.

Turning to the future, will the GRAMPIES defect to the cable and satellite services, the so-called new electronic media? Given the known formats of their programmes, this is doubtful. It may be dismissed as wishful thinking on the part of an established broadcaster, but evidence is already available that the GRAMPIES will be difficult to recruit for the new channels.

There is the evidence in the United Kingdom of the current pattern of use of video cassette recorders (Table 10.14). The over-55s, and particularly the over-65s, have been slow to adopt VCRs in the United Kingdom. Their overall level of ownership is still only 28 per cent and usage is overwhelmingly slanted to time-shifting existing broadcast material, and not to hiring prerecorded tapes from the high street shops. Less than one-fifth of the over-55s' viewing of VCR is to prerecorded material. The machines are being used, not to widen choice, but to reschedule the broadcast programmes at more convenient times. This points to a general satisfaction with what is already on offer.

Table 10.14   Video cassette recorder viewing

	All adults	Age group		
		16–54	55–64	Over-65
Own video cassette recorder (%)	55	68	48	16
Weekly hours				
Timeshift	3.3	3.4	2.6	4.0
Pre-recorded	1.8	2.0	0.9	0.6
Pre-recorded share (%)	35	37	26	13

Source: Television Omnibus Monitor, 1988

In conclusion, ITV is a very powerful medium for advertising to the GRAMPIES, as has been demonstrated, and it is likely to remain so for many years. They may not be quite so spritely as the under-55s group, and, as a totality, not quite so wealthy; but they are a marked forced in their own right, and are becoming more so. In the main, they are currently neglected by the advertiser relative to their commercial importance, despite being easy to reach on the 'box'. This neglect could be a major factor in determining why they do not remember and identify with advertising directed mainly at the young. Such careless omission is hard to understand in the context that most of the GRAMPIES will remain consumers of branded products for another 20–25 years. It will make marketing sense to pay them at least their due regard in future.

Appendix

Are people in your age group fitter and more healthy now than they used to be?
Much more so. You go to socials and local firms dances and always the older group are much more active. They seem to do more than the youngsters at these social functions. (60–65 Male C1)

Yes, they tend to get about more than they used to. I think compared with my parents, most certainly so. (60–65 Male C1)

Yes, believe it or not I do keep fit. I do my own keep-fit at home. I do a number of sit-ups and weight-training at home. I have some equipment and it keeps me in good shape. (55–60 Male C1)

There's so much going on for them now. They not included as old now. If you go to a leisure centre or a social or anything, age is irrespective—as long as you're healthy. (55–60 Female C2)

If I compare myself with my age group of say ten years ago, I think I am more fit and more active. (50–55 Male C1)

Very much, very much yes! I am very active, I played league tennis when I was 75—I'm more than that now! (75–80 Male AB)

Most of them seem to be hopping around. A lot of them are quite fit though. (Ex-Serviceman Chelsea Pensioner 75–80 Male C2)

I don't know. I feel fairly fit. For my view—I think they try to do everything they missed in their youth. (55–60 Female C1)

What do you do with yourself?
Well I do some voluntary work. (70–75 Female B)

Swim, play golf, go to classes at an education and art centre. (55–60 Female C1)

I don't find time hangs at all. I always find something to do. (70–75 Male C2)

Theatre mostly. I love watching theatre, I love going to theatre and I'm also involved in an amateur way because of a job. (60–65 Male B)

Scouting activities and I'm also involved in a local activity as well. (60–65 Male C1)

I work freelance anyway. I do a bit of writing and freelance selling. (55–60 Male C1)

Well I like the theatre and music. That's why I'm up here now getting some tickets for the Old Vic behind us. Reading mainly and usually eating and breathing! (55–60 Male C1)

Well I do craftwork—spinning wheels you know. (55–60 Female C2)

I swim everyday of my life. I play tennis and I admire my wife's gardening very much. I don't do much myself (75–80 Male AB)

I help other people mostly—do voluntary work and help people that I know. (60–65 Female D)

How about spending power. Do you think people in your age group have more money to spend than they used to?
We think so. We know that we appear to be slightly better off than we were a few years ago. (60–65 Male C1)

I think we are better off. (65–70 Male C2)

I think so, more so now. Most have been sensible—they've been in pension schemes. (55–60 Female C2)

Well the money we've got is ours now. You don't have to fork out on the children all the time. (60–65 Female C1)

Do you have savings as well then?
Well we try to save, yes. (60–65 Female C1)

What about stocks and shares and things like that?
We dabble. (60–65 Female C1)

We don't do too much of investing in shares—it's mostly savings certificates, the building society, though my husband does a little in shares. (70–75 Female AB)

Most of my money is tied up in property—my own property in fact. (55–60 Male C1)

Well I don't want the tax people to listen, but I've got a little savings on the side yes. (60–65 Male C1)

What about holidays. Do you get the chance to go away at all?
I've been to Majorca. I've been practically everywhere the charter planes go, but I've been on the cheap ones. (60–65 Male D)

We've been taking one holiday a year, but as we're both now over 70, we're going to take two a year. Short ones not long ones! (70–75 Male AB)

I can afford one overseas holiday a year—which isn't bad really. (55–60 Female C1)

I prefer to stay at home, my wife prefers to go abroad. So we compromise with one of each usually. (60–65 Male C1)

Majorca. We go to Majorca quite a bit. Northern Majorca—Alcudia is a very nice spot. It's away from the rabble. (55–60 Male C1)

Well we used to go twice a year at one time, sometime around February and then sometime about September. (55–60 Male C2)

Usually one in the Spring and one in the Summer. (65–70 Male—Wealthy American tourist)

I think the Winter holidays for old age pensioners/senior citizens are very good in so far as they are warm. They don't suffer from rheumatism and other illnesses old age people get and those three months holidays are good, very, very good. (60–65 Male D)

And what about a drink. Do you enjoy a tipple?
I don't drink. (55–60 Male C2)

Champagne—when we can afford it. If we could afford it all the time we'd drink nothing but champagne. (60–65 Male B)

Whisky 'n American and that sort of thing. (60–65 Male C1)

Wine—white wine, scotch and ginger ale on the rocks. (55–60 Male C1)

Guinness, because I was weaned on Guinness and I worked for them for many, many years. (70–75 Male C1)

I prefer whisky and a good lager but not together! (60–65 Male Wealthy American tourist)

Do you get the chance to watch much television?
All the time. (60–65 Female D)

I watch one or two programmes yes. A wide variety of stuff. (55–60 Male C1)

We're selective. There's certain things that we definitely like and other things we don't watch at all. (70–75 Female AB)

What sort of programmes then?
Well, we like quiz programmes, wildlife programmes, travel programmes. (70–75 Female AB)

Certain sports and wildlife programmes and that's the lot. (70–75 Male C2)

These comedies you know. Palladium shows—Jimmy Tarbuck. (55–60 Male C2)

The best one is Michael Aspel. I think he's the best person on television. (55–60 Female C2)

Political programmes. Sunday mornings on independent television. (60–65 Male C1)

Child's Play—that's one of our favourite programmes. (70–75 Female AB)

Animal programmes or sport. (60–65 Male C1)

Sport mostly. (60–65 Male C1)

I hate sport programmes. (55–60 Female C2)

What about television commercials. What sort of impact do you think they have on people?
I have been persuaded by VW advertising that they tend to last longer, therefore we bought that. (60–65 Male B)

To some degree, especially my wife. (60–65 Male C1)

I watch the adverts on television but I make my own judgements on things you know. (60–65 Male C1)

Yes, I've bought quite a few things just to see what they're like. (55–60 Female D)

It has some influence in the sense of information—the sort of things that are available to buy. (55–60 Male C1)

References

AGB Attwood, ITVA Availability-To-View Survey April, 1984
Gallup Poll, Social Surveys Limited, 1987
ITV Television Omnibus Monitors conducted by National Opinion Polls, 1980 onwards
JICNARS, National Readership Survey 1987
Journal of Advertising Research (USA), 'The portrayal of older Americans in television commercials, Swayne & Greco, 1987
LWT, Analysis of Commercial Content, August 1988
LWT, Commercial Recognition Surveys, conducted by Marplan, 1987
LWT Outstanding Advertisement Surveys conducted by BMRB, 1986, 1987, 1988
LWT street interviews, Waterloo area, autumn 1988

11
Conclusions
Dr Stephan Buck

In my more philosophical moments, I sometimes feel that the main problem with the world is not that matters are obscure or impossible to predict, but that it is difficult to change the pattern of events even when they are clear and, more important, clearly undesirable.

Contrary to popular opinion, most marketers are not particularly adventurous, forward looking or trend-setting. Like most of us, they are happiest following their normal pattern of activities in the way they are used to. The result of this is that any new marketing idea tends to face a highly predictable three-stage process.

The first stage is the flat assertion that the new idea is simply unnecessary. There has never been any call for it, there never will be, and it is a sheer waste of time thinking about it.

Eventually, this simple rejection turns into a more complex assessment of the position. The argument then goes that the idea may well be interesting, but unfortunately it is impractical. It would indeed be desirable to do this, but everyone knows it could not work.

Finally, the idea reaches a cusp, a point of radical change, when from being unnecessary or impossible, it becomes totally obvious and easy almost overnight. But this, too, raises problems. Marketing ideas which look difficult usually look so because they are difficult. The airy assumption that now we have seen the relevance of the idea, we can simply sail in and make it work, very often leads to tears before bed time. But the consequences can be even more unfortunate. If a few marketers, having launched into a new idea, ill-prepared and ill-advised, fail, the remainder, who had probably spent years denying the validity of the concept altogether, can then happily relax, say, 'I told you so', and the whole process returns to square one.

The recognition of the ageing population as a significant market provides an excellent example of the process I have just outlined. As little as five years ago, the idea of selling anything to old people, except a few patent medicines or 'Granny Bonds', was simply ignored. It was generally accepted that there was no market there, and indeed, any attempt to suggest the real wealth of many old people was often treated as a vicious attack on the aged poor, and a call to cut pensions.

We have undoubtedly moved a long way over the past few years. The idea that the old could constitute a significant market is now probably accepted by most marketers. But the majority are probably still of the opinion that the old do not constitute a target market suitable for their particular products or services, and that no adaptation would be possible to change this fact.

One of the major purposes of this book has been to cast doubt on such conveniently simple beliefs. In Chapters 5 and 6 we saw the present purchasing patterns of the old, the way in which some skilful marketers have built highly successful businesses by taking advantage of actual or potential demand, and we discussed where opportunities still do not appear to have been grasped, and what lessons could be learnt particularly from the United States. Similarly, Chapters 5, 9 and 10 looked at ways in which marketers could most effectively reach old people generally or particular target groups among the old.

I hope that this function is useful as it stands, and would by itself justify the book. But there is another and, I think, even more timely purpose to be served. If we return to the three-stage process that I discussed earlier, I suspect that the view of the old as a market is now just about on the cusp between being impossible and being easy. Already, the advertising agencies, always a good indicator of which way the wind of fashion is blowing, are coming up with their list of smart acronyms for older people, the GLAMS, the WOOPIES, etc., and using them to put over the message of the fantastic market which awaits lucky advertisers among the older age groups. The trouble is that it pays people trying to arouse interest in the older age groups as a market to make it all sound childishly simple: 'We have just discovered this splendid target group of consumers and now we will show you how to sell your product to them.'

Unfortunately, it is not that easy, and another function of this book is to explain why not, and to point to some of the pitfalls which might await the unwary marketer. The older-age market is heavily polarized, consisting of many people with considerable wealth, but also containing many other people of very limited means. Also, to a considerable extent it does consist of people heavy in capital but light in income. It certainly involves people whose formative years were spent during the great depression and the austerity of World War, and whose attitudes to spending derive from that fact, as Monty Alexander points out in Chapter 7. These are not reasons for ignoring the market, but they do explain the necessity for a careful and well-thought-out approach.

This would not claim to be a 'How to' book. When you have finished reading it, you will not be in a position to go out immediately and sell goods to the old. But I like to think it is at least a 'How to find out how to' book. It is designed to show the sort of marketing groundwork that is needed, and is available, to break into what is inevitably a difficult but potentially highly rewarding market.

Index